PRACTICAL ILLUSTRATIONS

1 Peter
2 Peter
1 John
2 John
3 John
Jude

Leadership Ministries Worldwide
Chattanooga, TN

Practical Illustrations has been compiled for God's people to use both in their personal lives and in their teaching. Leadership Ministries Worldwide wants God's people to use *Practical Illustrations*. The purpose of the copyright is to prevent the reproduction, misuse, and abuse of the material.

May our Lord bless us all as we live, preach, teach, and write for Him, fulfilling His great commission to live righteous and godly lives and to make disciples of all nations.

Please address all requests for information or permission to:
Leadership Ministries Worldwide
PO Box 21310
Chattanooga, TN 37424-0310
Ph.# (423) 855-2181 FAX (423) 855-8616 E-Mail info@outlinebible.org
http://www.outlinebible.org

Library of Congress Catalog Card Number: 2001-135015
International Standard Book Number: 1-57407-187-4

PRINTED IN THE U.S.A.

PUBLISHED BY LEADERSHIP MINISTRIES WORLDWIDE

1 2 3 4 5 12 13 14 15 16

LEADERSHIP MINISTRIES WORLDWIDE

DEDICATED

To all the men and women of the world who preach and teach the Gospel of our Lord Jesus Christ and to the Mercy and Grace of God

- Demonstrated to us in Christ Jesus our Lord.

  "In whom we have redemption through His blood, the forgiveness of sins, according to the riches of His grace." (Eph. 1:7)

- Out of the mercy and grace of God His Word has flowed. Let every person know that God will have mercy upon him, forgiving and using him to fulfill His glorious plan of salvation.

  "For God so loved the world, that he gave His only begotten Son, that whosoever believeth in Him should not perish, but have everlasting life. For God sent not his son into the world to condemn the world, but that the world through him might be saved." (Jn. 3:16-17)

  "For this is good and acceptable in the sight of God our Saviour; who will have all men to be saved, and to come unto the knowledge of the truth." (1 Tim. 2:3-4)

9/09

Practical Illustrations

has been compiled for God's servants to use in their study, teaching, and preaching of God's Holy Word...

- To share the Word of God with the world.
- To help the believer, both minister and layman alike, in his understanding, preaching, and teaching of God's Word.
- To do everything we possibly can to lead men, women, boys and girls to give their hearts and lives to Jesus Christ and to secure the eternal life which He offers.
- To do all we can to minister to the needy of the world.
- To give Jesus Christ His proper place, the place the Word gives Him. Therefore, no work of Leadership Ministries Worldwide will ever be personalized.

About
Practical Illustrations

This volume of *Practical Illustrations* covers 1 and 2 Peter, 1, 2 and 3 John, and Jude. You can use it alone or as a companion to other *Outline Bible* Resource Materials. This book is cross-indexed several ways to make it easy to find the illustrations you need. The following information is provided to help you use the book more effectively:

Use this index if you want to find illustrations for a particular passage of Scripture.

Each illustration or introduction includes the following elements to aid in your study and in locating the appropriate illustration, whether by topic or Scripture reference:

Key Number: Each illustration is numbered. The first digit indicates the *Practical Illustrations* volume number (which is the same as the corresponding volume of *The Preacher's Outline and Sermon Bible*®). The second digit indicates the order in which the illustration appears in *Practical Illustrations.*

Subject Heading: Each illustration is categorized by topic.

Scripture Reference: Each illustration is keyed to the Scripture passage it illustrates.

POSB Reference: This indicates where additional information can be found in *The Preacher's Outline and Sermon Bible*®.

Illustration Title: Each illustration is given an appropriate title.

Use this index if you want to find illustrations on a particular topic.

Scripture Index

1 PETER

REFERENCE **ILLUSTRATIONS**

I Peter	Subject	Title	Num.	Pg.
1:1-2	Attitude	Keep a Good Attitude	12–109	17
1:1-2	Christian Life	Trusting in God's Grace	12–114	20
1:1-2	Heaven	The Believer's Eternal Home	12–145	40
1:3-5	Assurance	The Comfort of God's Guiding Hand	12–104	15
1:3-5	Hope	The Ability to Keep Hope Alive	12–149	42
1:6-9	Trials	Gathering Your Strength	12–221	83
1:6-9	Trials	In All Things Give Thanks	12–222	84
1:10-12	Grace	The Great Mercy of God	12–142	37
1:10-12	Salvation	God's Wondrous Plan of Salvation	12–207	75
1:13-16	Holy–Holiness	Staying Pure in an Impure World	12–146	40
1:13-16	Obedience	Getting Rid of Selfish Desires	12–179	59
1:17-21	Respect	Showing Proper Reverence	12–199	70
1:17-21	Resurrection	Only God Can Give Life	12–200	71
1:22-25	Priorities	The Importance of Eternal Things	12–195	68
1:22-25	Pure - Purity	Caring for Those You Love	12–197	69
2:1-3	Sin	Adopting a Zero-Tolerance Policy	12–212	78
2:1-3	Word of God	The Great Value of God's Word	12–231	89
2:1-3	Worldliness	Our Desperate Need for Cleansing	12–239	94
2:4-8	Christian Life	The Strength of Community	12–113	19
2:4-8	Jesus Christ	Build on the Sure Foundation	12–158	48
2:4-8	Jesus Christ	The Danger of Rejecting Christ	12–159	48
2:4-8	Pride	The Foolishness of Opposing God	12–194	67
2:9-10	Mercy	Who Will Pay for Your Sin?	12–177	58
2:9-10	Salvation	Opening the Floodgates of Praise	12–209	76
2:11-12	Conviction	Being Heavenly-Minded	12–120	24
2:11-12	Lust	The Overpowering Grip of Lust	12–175	57
2:11-12	Witness–Witnessing	A Life-Impacting Faith	12–228	87
2:13-17	Citizenship	The Believer's Influence in the World	12–115	20
2:13-17	Submission	The Protection of God	12–218	82
2:18-20	Persecution	Breaking the Bonds of Sin	12–190	65
2:18-20	Work	Giving Your Best for the Lord	12–235	91
2:18-20	Work	Searching for God's Blessings	12–236	92
2:21-25	Jesus Christ	No One Ever Cared Like Jesus	12–160	49
2:21-25	Repentance	How to Be Debt Free	12–198	70
2:21-25	Suffering	The Mark of a Genuine Christian	12–219	82
3:1-6	Marriage	Actions Preach Louder Than Words	12–176	58
3:1-6	Witness–Witnessing	The Testimony of Our Lives	12–230	88

1 PETER

REFERENCE **ILLUSTRATIONS**

2 Peter

Reference **Illustrations**

2 Peter	Subject	Title	Num.	Pg.
1:1-4	Born Again	Transformed to New Life	12–111	18
1:1-4	Peace	Jesus Christ: The Source of Peace	12–185	62
1:5-15	Legacy	Touching Others for Christ	12–164	51
1:5-15	Love	The Power of Sacrificial Love	12–172	56
1:16-21	Salvation	The Greatness of Christ	12–208	76
1:16-21	Word of God	Obeying God's Word	12–232	90
2:1-9	False Teachers	Heed the Warning Signs	12–131	31
2:1-9	False Teachers	Warning: Avoid Self-Exaltation	12–134	33
2:10-22	False Teachers	Keeping Your Guard Up	12–132	31
2:10-22	Judgment	God Cannot Be Mocked	12–163	51
3:1-7	Judgment	The Danger of Ignorance	12–162	50
3:1-7	Lust	Living on the Brink of Disaster	12–174	57
3:8-10	Jesus Christ	Are You Ready for His Return?	12–155	46
3:11-14	Witness–Witnessing	Evidence You Can Depend Upon	12–227	87
3:15-18	Grace	Sharing the Good News	12–143	38
3:15-18	Obedience	Beware—Lest You Stray	12–178	59

1 JOHN

REFERENCE **ILLUSTRATIONS**

1 John	Subject	Title	Num.	Pg.
1:1-5	Fellowship	The Loving Reach of God	12–137	35
1:1-5	Light	Jesus Is the Light of the World	12–166	52
1:6-7	Forgiveness	Clean on the Inside	12–139	36
1:6-7	Light	Exposing the Darkness	12–165	52
1:8-9	Sin	Confession Is Good for the Soul	12–213	79
1:10–2:2	Righteousness	Owning Up to the Truth	12–202	72
1:10–2:2	Jesus Christ	Our Judge and Our Savior	12–161	49
2:3-6	Commitment	Putting Others Before Self	12–117	22
2:3-6	Obedience	Keeping God's Word	12–180	60
2:7-11	Obedience	The Need to Be Accountable	12–181	60
2:7-11	Worldliness	Hatred Is Blind	12–238	93
2:12–14	Word of God	Our Source of Spiritual Strength	12–233	90
2:12–24	Spiritual Warfare	Living On a Higher Plane	12–216	80
2:15-17	Commitment	Remaining True to Your Word	12–116	21
2:15-17	Obedience	The Path to Safety	12–183	61
2:18-23	False Teachers	Beware False Teachers Within the Church	12–128	29
2:18-23	Word of God	Protection Against Deadly Doctrine	12–234	91
2:24-27	Gospel	Abiding in Christ—a Way of Life	12–141	37
2:24-27	Holy Spirit	The Abiding Presence of God	12–147	41
2:28-29	Abide–Abiding	The Results of Faithfulness	12–101	13
2:28-29	Righteousness	The Power to Live Righteously	12–203	73
3:1-3	Godliness	The Secret to Holiness	12–140	36
3:1-3	Love	The Comfort of God's Love	12–167	53
3:4-9	Salvation	Acknowledging Your Sin and Your Savior	12–204	73
3:4-9	Salvation	Freed from a Life of Sin	12–206	75
3:10-17	Love	Getting Rid of Anger	12–169	54
3:10-17	Love	Willing to Take the Risk	12–173	56
3:18-24	Holy Spirit	The Source of Abundant Life	12–148	41
4:1-6	False Teaching	Trying the Spirits	12–135	33
4:1-6	Worldliness	Deadly Necessities	12–237	92
4:7-21	Love	Focusing on People	12–168	53
4:7-21	Witness–Witnessing	The Proof of Love	12–229	88
5:1-5	Faith	The Power to Overcome	12–127	28
5:1-5	Obedience	Nothing Else Will Do	12–182	61
5:6-8	Evangelism	We Have a Mission	12–126	27
5:6-8	Salvation	Falling into His Grace	12–205	74

1 JOHN

REFERENCE **ILLUSTRATIONS**

1 John	Subject	Title	Num.	Pg.
5:9-15	Assurance	Knowing You Are Heaven-Bound	12–105	15
5:9-15	Jesus Christ	Believing What You Hear	12–156	47
5:9-15	Truth	Facing the Facts	12–223	85
5:16-21	Prayer	Interceding for the Flock	12–192	66
5:16-21	Sin	Dropping a Few Pounds	12–214	79

2 JOHN

REFERENCE **ILLUSTRATIONS**

2 John	Subject	Title	Num.	Pg.
1-4	Call of God	Allowing God to Use You	12–112	19
1-4	Discipleship	Leading Others to Walk in Truth	12–124	26
5-6	Love	Love Your Enemies	12–170	55
5-6	Love	Putting Love into Action	12–171	55
7-13	Deception	Beware of Deceivers	12–122	25
7-13	Deception	Guard Your Reward	12–123	26
7-13	False Teaching	Truth—the Safeguard Against Cults	12–136	34

3 JOHN

REFERENCE **ILLUSTRATIONS**

3 John	Subject	Title	Num.	Pg.
1-8	Prosperity	The True Measure of Success	12–196	69
1-8	Service	Investing Wisely in Others	12–210	77
9-14	Association	Choose Your Models Carefully	12–102	13
9-14	Testimony	Always Being Watched	12–220	83

JUDE

REFERENCE **ILLUSTRATIONS**

Jude	Subject	Title	Num.	Pg.
1-2	Growth, Christian	Keep Pressing On	12–144	39
1-2	Humility	The Secret of Success	12–154	45
3-10	False Teachers	Prepare to Face the Enemy	12–133	32
3-16	False Teachers	Empty Promises Leading Nowhere	12–130	30
3-16	False Teachers	The Consequences of Deception	12–129	29
3-16	Flattery	Words Without Sincerity	12–138	35
17-25	Assurance	Secure In God's Hands	12–103	14
17-25	Witness–Witnessing	Caring Enough to Share	12–225	86

PRACTICAL ILLUSTRATIONS

PRACTICAL ILLUSTRATIONS

12–101

ABIDE–ABIDING

1 John 2:28-29

The Results of Faithfulness

(POSB, Note 1)

Abiding in Christ will always produce fruit, even though it is not always apparent. Here is the story of a man who produced glorious fruit in a very unspectacular way.

> A century and a half ago there died a humble minister in a small village in Leicestershire, England. He had never attended college and had no degrees. He was merely a faithful village minister. In his congregation was a young cobbler to whom he gave special attention, teaching him the Word of God.
>
> This young man was later to be renowned as William Carey, one of the greatest missionaries of modern times. This same minister had a son, a boy whom he taught faithfully, and constantly encouraged. The boy's character and powers were profoundly affected by his father's life. That son was Robert Hall, the mightiest public orator of his day, whose sermons influenced the decisions of statesmen and whose character was as saintly as his preaching was phenomenal. [By comparison,] it seemed that the village pastor [had] accomplished little. There were no spectacular revivals, but his faithful witness and godly life had much to do with giving India its Carey and England its Robert Hall.[1]

You do not have to be famous, wealthy, or even educated to faithfully abide in Christ. God expects every believer to live for Him wherever He has placed him in life—regardless of the circumstances. Keep on abiding in Christ—who knows *who* you will reach for Christ.

12–102

ASSOCIATION

3 John 9-14

Choose Your Models Carefully

(POSB, Note 1, point 6)

It is easy—even natural—to be in awe of someone who seems to have it all together. But we must be careful to follow only those who have godly character.

---

1 *Sunday School Times.* Walter B. Knight. *Knight's Master Book of 4,000 Illustrations.* (Grand Rapids, MI: Eerdmans Publishing Company, 1994), p.318.

In *Sports Spectrum,* Harold Reynolds, ESPN baseball analyst and one-time all-star second baseman for the Seattle Mariners, writes:

> When I was growing up in Corvallis, Oregon, there was [a basketball] player named Gus Williams. Gus tied his shoes in back instead of in front like normal. I thought that was so cool. So I started tying my shoes in the back. I wanted to be like Gus. He wore number 10; I wore number 10. He wore one wrist band; I wore one wrist band.
>
> One day I was lying in bed and my stomach was killing me. I noticed that it wasn't my sports hero, Gus Williams, who came to my room to take care of me.
>
> It was my mother.
>
> That's when I began to understand the difference between heroes and role models. I stopped looking at athletic accomplishments to determine who I wanted to pattern my life after. Instead, I tried to emulate people with strong character who were doing things of lasting value.
>
> Whom we look up to largely determines who we become. Choose your heroes well.[2]

12–103

ASSURANCE

1 Peter 1:3-5

(POSB, Note 3, point 2)

The Comfort of God's Guiding Hand

How sure are you about eternal life? Do you really trust God to protect you? To guide you safely to heaven? Does your faith work in everyday life?

Young Cindy and her mother spent a good portion of the day shopping at a mall, with Cindy's attention leaping from one exciting thing to another. All day long, Cindy and her mother held hands and enjoyed being together. Cindy knew she was in good hands, so she never questioned her mother's leading as they shopped.

When the day of shopping came to an end, the young child and her mother left the mall to walk to the parking lot. Suddenly, Cindy stopped and stared at the sea of cars, cars of every type and color as far as the eye could see. "Mommy, what will we do? How will we ever find our car?"

With swift assurance, the mother lovingly replied, "Cindy, you trusted me to take care of you this far. Don't you believe I can get you safely home?" Cindy thought for a moment, then said with a peaceful smile, "I don't understand how, but I believe you, Mommy."

As believers, we cannot always see the way home. We too must trust our Heavenly Father to keep us safe in this world—and keep on trusting Him day by day. Then one day, Christ will return to take us home. He will not leave us stranded in this world.

---

2 Craig Brian Larson. *Choice Contemporary Stories & Illustrations.* (Grand Rapids, MI: Baker Books, 1998), p. 232.

PRACTICAL ILLUSTRATIONS

12–104

ASSURANCE

1 Peter 5:10-14

(POSB, Note 1)

God Will Undergird the Believer

By trusting in God, we can go far beyond what we could ever do on our own.

In a sermon, Juan Carlos Ortiz spoke of a conversation with a circus trapeze artist. The performer admitted the net underneath was there to keep them from breaking their necks, but added, "The net also keeps us from falling. Imagine there is no net. We would be so nervous that we would be more likely to miss and fall. If there wasn't a net, we would not dare to do some of the things we do. But because there's a net, we dare to make two turns, and once I made three turns—thanks to the net!"

Ortiz makes this observation: "We have security in God. When we are sure in his arms, we dare to attempt big things for God. We dare to be holy. We dare to be obedient. We dare, because we know the eternal arms of God will hold us if we fall."[3]

And what if *you* fall? Do you have God as your safety net?

12–105

ASSURANCE

1 Peter 5:1-4

(POSB, Note 3, point 2)

Heaven's Reward

For every believer who has been faithful, God has promised a crown of glory.

The story is told of the suffering in Russia many years ago; how the Christians were persecuted and imprisoned: Some gave up Christianity and their faith in Christ and were freed. Others chose to suffer, "not accepting deliverance." The story went on to tell of seventy who had been imprisoned for a long time, underfed, and at last taken out, thinly clad, one cold winter night, to a lake of ice where they were left to die.

A Russian guard was in charge of them. He was warmly clad, and properly fed and did not mind the cold. However he seemed to see the prisoners fall one by one on the ice, and as one fell it seemed as if the heavens opened and an angel appeared with a golden crown. Then another would fall and another angel appeared with another golden crown.

It seemed as if they had nearly all fallen, and the Russian guard, thinking he must be in a trance or a dream, aroused himself and found all had fallen save one.

That one called to him, and said: "Oh, sir, save my life, I'm dying! I'll not be a Christian, anything, only save my life."

"Quick," said the Russian guard, "change clothes with me." And he stepped out on the ice. He had seen that there was one more angel and one more golden crown.[4]

Will you serve the Lord faithfully to the end? Then God has a crown for you!

---

3 Craig B. Larson, Editor. *Illustrations for Preaching & Teaching*,. (Grand Rapids, MI: Baker Books, 1993), p.215.

4 *Courtesy Moody Monthly*. Walter B. Knight. *3,000 Illustrations for Christian Service*. (Grand Rapids, MI: Eerdmans Publishing Company, 1971), p.570.

12–106

ASSURANCE

1 Peter 3:18-22

Hope in Christ

(POSB, Note 2, point 2)

The triumph of Christ means that we have a guarantee of eternal life—even in the face of physical death.

> Years ago a submarine sank....As soon as possible divers descended. They walked about the disabled ship endeavoring to find some signs of life within. At last they heard a gentle tapping. Listening intently they recognized the dots and dashes of the Morse code. These were the words spelled out, "Is there hope?"
>
> "IS THERE HOPE?" This is the constant cry of humanity, and Easter is the answer to that cry."[5]

Is there hope? There is if you allow Christ to enter through the door of your heart.

12–107

ASSURANCE

1 John 5:9-15

Knowing You Are Heaven-Bound

(POSB, Note 2, point 1)

One of the great pillars of the Christian life is the complete assurance that God gives His children. It is an assurance that is not bound to our fragile circumstances. God's assurance is founded upon the finished work of His Son on the cross. Does this kind of assurance work...even when death looms?

> An aged lady left Buffalo by boat for Cleveland, Ohio, to visit a daughter. A terrible storm arose, and the passengers, fearing death, gathered for prayer. But the aged lady seemed quite unconcerned.
>
> She sat praising the Lord. Some of the passengers, after the storm subsided, became curious to know the reason for the old lady's calmness. They gathered around her and asked her the secret.
>
> "Well, children," she replied, "It is like this. I had two daughters. One died and went home to Heaven; the other moved to Cleveland. When the storm arose, I wondered which daughter I might visit first, the one in Cleveland or the one in Heaven, and I was quite unconcerned as to which."[6]

If you have already received eternal life, you, too, need not fear what fate is awaiting you around the corner.

---

5 Walter B. Knight. *Knight's Master Book of 4,000 Illustrations,* p.557.

6 *Wesleyan Methodist.* Walter B. Knight. *Knight's Master Book of 4,000 Illustrations,* p.14.

PRACTICAL ILLUSTRATIONS

12–108

ASSURANCE

Jude 17-25

(POSB, Note 4, point 5)

Secure In God's Hands

We live in a world where few things are sure: there is little security and life is ever so brief. But one thing you can count on is the constant care of the One who keeps you in the hollow of His hand. Through every generation, believers have found themselves in the same position—in the loving hands of the Savior. Yours is the same great privilege as Martin Luther's.

> When Martin Luther was in the throes of the Reformation and the Pope was trying to bring him back to the Catholic church, he sent a cardinal to deal with Luther and buy him with gold.
>
> The cardinal wrote to the Pope, "The fool does not love gold." The cardinal, when he could not convince Luther, said to him, "What do you think the Pope cares for the opinions of a German...[farmer]? The Pope's little finger is stronger than all Germany. Do you expect your princes to take up arms to defend you—you, a wretched worm like you? I tell you no. And where will you be then?"
>
> Luther's reply was simple. "Where I am now. In the hands of Almighty God."[7]

Place your confidence in God. He will keep you by His power.

12–109

ATTITUDE

1 Peter 1:1-2

(POSB, Introduction)

Keep a Good Attitude

What attitude should believers have when persecution and suffering comes to them? To be honest, many of us are quick to complain to God when we are persecuted. Believers constantly need to be reminded that nothing comes our way without first passing through the caring hands of Christ. Listen to the story of these two optimists:

> A certain organization offer[ed]...a bounty of $5,000 for wolves captured alive. It turned Sam and Jed into fortune hunters. Day and night they scoured the mountains and forests looking for their valuable prey.
>
> Exhausted one night, they fell asleep dreaming of their potential fortune. Suddenly, Sam awoke to see that they were surrounded by about fifty wolves with flaming eyes and bared teeth. He nudged his friend and said, "Jed, wake up! We're rich!"[8]

When persecution and suffering surround you, an unshakable assurance of your salvation can turn the worst situation into an opportunity for your good and God's glory.

---

7 *Pentecostal Herald.* Walter B. Knight. *Knight's Master Book of 4,000 Illustrations*, p.19.

8 Craig B. Larson. *Illustrations for Preaching & Teaching*, p. 12.

Practical Illustrations

12–110

Backsliding

1 Peter 3:7

The Danger of Worldly Associations

(POSB, Note 3, point 1)

It is the Christian man's awesome responsibility to protect the faith of his wife. A man is truly blessed to have a wife who fears the Lord and he should take special care to preserve that blessing.

> "Mark Twain" was the pen name of Samuel Clements [sic]. As a young man he fell in love with a beautiful Christian girl named Livy and married her. Being devoted to her Lord, she wanted a family altar and prayer at meals after she and Sam were married. This was done for a time and then one day Sam said, "Livy, you can go on with this by yourself if you want to but leave me out. I don't believe in your God and you're only making a hypocrite out of me."
>
> Fame and affluence came. There were court appearances in Europe. Sam and Livy were riding high and Livy got farther and farther away from her early devotion to her Lord. The eventual fall came. In an hour of bitter need Sam Clements said, "Livy, if your Christian faith can help you now, turn to it." Livy replied, "I can't Sam; I haven't any; it was destroyed a long time ago."[9]

How would you like to stand before God one day in Samuel Clemen's shoes? Men, keep the channels of prayer open by honoring your wives.

12–111

Born Again

2 Peter 1:1-4

Transformed to New Life

(POSB, Note 5)

When we are born again, we leave behind the corruption that devastated our souls. This corruption is not found only in those who come out of dark gutters. It applies to everyone—even you.

> In England there is a paper factory that makes the finest stationery in the world. One day a man touring the factory asked what [the stationery] was made from. He was shown a huge pile of old rags and told that the rag content was what determined the quality of the paper. The visitor wouldn't believe it. In weeks he received from the company a package of paper with his initials embossed on it. On the top piece were written the words "Dirty rags transformed."
>
> The same is true of the Christian life. It is a process of transformation from what we were into something new and wonderful.[10]

> **"But we are all as an unclean *thing,* and all our righteousnesses *are* as filthy rags; and we all do fade as a leaf; and our iniquities, like the wind, have taken us away" (Is.64:6).**

Being born again is the only remedy for the terrible filth of sin's corruption.

9 Dr. Paul S. James, in *Christian Digest.* Walter B. Knight. *Knight's Master Book of 4,000 Illustrations*, p.299.

10 Michael P. Green. *Illustrations for Biblical Preaching.* (Grand Rapids, MI: Baker Books, 1996), p.81.

Practical Illustrations

12–112

Call of God

2 John 1-4

(POSB, Note 1, point 2)

Allowing God to Use You

When God calls a person, He sets that person apart, chooses the person to be His follower. There is no greater joy than to be set apart, to be a true follower of God.

> [Felix] Mendelssohn, it is said, once visited the cathedral at Fridbourg, and, having heard the great organ, went into the organ loft and asked to be allowed to play it. The old organist, in jealousy for his instrument, at first refused, but was afterward prevailed on to allow the great German composer to try the colossal "thunder" of the cathedral.
>
> And after standing by in an ecstasy of delight and amazement for a few moments, he suddenly laid his hands on the shoulders of the inspired musician and exclaimed: "Who are you? What is your name?" "Mendelssohn," replied the player. "And can it be! that I had so nearly refused to let Mendelssohn touch this organ!"
>
> How little the Lord's people know what they are doing when they refuse to let Christ have full possession of their entire life and evoke the full melody and harmony of which it is capable![11]

12–113

Christian Life

1 Peter 2:4-8

(POSB, Note 2, point 1)

The Strength of Community

William Barclay tells a story about the ancient Greek city of Sparta and then drives the point home with a striking application.

> There is a famous story from Sparta. A Spartan king boasted to a visiting monarch about the walls of Sparta. The visiting monarch looked around and he could see no walls. He said to the Spartan king, "Where are these walls about which you speak and boast so much?" The Spartan king pointed at his bodyguard of magnificent Spartan troops. "These," he said, "are the walls of Sparta, and every man of them a brick."
>
> Now, the point is quite clear. So long as a brick lies by itself it is useless. It only becomes of use when it is built into a building. That is why it was made; and it is in being built into a building that it realizes its function and the reason for its existence. It is so with the individual Christian. To realize his destiny he must not remain alone, but must be built into the fabric and edifice of the Church.[12]

---

11 *Gospel Herald.* Walter B. Knight. *Knight's Master Book of 4,000 Illustrations,* p.109.

12 William Barclay. *The Letters of James and Peter.* "Daily Study Bible Series." (Philadelphia, PA: Westminster Press), p.231.

12–114

CHRISTIAN LIFE

1 Peter 1:1-2

(POSB, Note 5)

Trusting in God's Grace

It was the remarkable Helen Keller who once said that life is either a daring experience or nothing. Being blind, deaf, and dumb, she knew better than anyone the special challenges people face every day. Those who take on the world without experiencing God's grace and peace are doomed to failure, to a life that amounts to nothing.

> A Georgia farmer, ragged and barefooted, was standing on the steps of his tumble-down shack. A stranger stopped for a drink of water. "How is your cotton coming along?" he asked. "Ain't got none," replied the farmer. "Didn't you plant any?" asked the stranger. "Nope," was the reply,
>
> "Afraid of bollweevils."
>
> "Well," continued the stranger, "how is your corn?" "Didn't plant none," came the answer, "fraid there weren't gonna to be no rain."
>
> The visitor persevered: "Well, how are your potatoes?" "Ain't got none. Scairt of potato bugs."
>
> "Really, what did you plant?" pressed the stranger. "Nothing," was the calm reply, "I jest played [it] safe."[13]

Have you been "playing it safe"? It's time to trust God to provide all your needs, time to tackle life with gusto, experiencing the fullness of God's grace and peace!

12–115

CITIZENSHIP

1 Peter 2:13-17

(POSB, Note 2, point 3)

The Believer's Influence in the World

God has given His people a decree to take the gospel into every area of their culture, including *government*. For far too long, believers have withdrawn from government. The result has been catastrophic. Laws have passed that are filled with the thinking of the world. Biblical ideas are considered closed-minded. Is it easy to get involved in the political process? Not always. Secular forces will oppose you every step along the way. Here is one believer's story: a citizen who feared God more than man.

> A young Christian man wanted to get involved in the political process on the precinct level. A committed Christian, he realized he had certain civic responsibilities. In no way did his Christian commitment exempt him from becoming a part of the solution to government's challenges. He knew that he should influence his world for good wherever possible, including the realm of politics. He voted and encouraged others to do the same. But he felt God leading him further, to take a particular stand for the truths taught in the Bible.

---

13 Ted Kyle and John Todd. *A Treasury of Bible Illustrations.* (Chattanooga, TN: AMG International, 1995), p. 374.

At the end of what he thought was a smooth public meeting, he made it a point to greet a man who had taught him in school. Outstretching his hand to his former teacher, he was repelled by a barrage of profanity directed toward him. "You blankety-blank Christians have no business in politics. You can't legislate your narrow-minded morality and impose it on the rest of us. Keep your religion in the church and leave the job of politics to the experts!" The young man privately thanked God that he was counted worthy to suffer persecution for the sake of the gospel.

What creates this kind of violent reaction to Christians who get involved in politics? Is it an attempt by Satan to keep the believer behind the walls of the church building? There is no question, if we choose to be the church outside our walls, we become a direct threat to the schemes of the devil. The choice is simple: we can fear confrontation with the devil's agents, or we can obey and fear God. We cannot do both.

12–116

COMMITMENT

1 John 2:3-6

(POSB, Note 4)

Putting Others Before Self

People are crying out for living examples of commitment to convictions. Unbelievers are growing weary of Christians who fail to live up to what they preach and teach. But, take hope. There are still believers who practice what they preach.

The president of a large organization was well known in many countries. In the world's eyes, he had it all: fame and a guaranteed job for life.

His wife of many years, however, had become so ill that she required constant attention. Advice came freely. "Put her in a nursing home ... Hire a live-in nurse ... Put your work first." But this gracious man of God refused this kind of advice. Being financially able, he made the decision to resign to take care of his wife himself.

After he resigned, he was asked over and over, "Why did you give up such a wonderful opportunity?" "Give up a wonderful opportunity? You do not understand. God has sent a wonderful opportunity my way. I count it a privilege that I am the best person on the face of the earth to minister to my wife. She needs me...and I need her. Other men can take over the organization, but only I can take care of her."

This man's act of responsibility did more in one day to show commitment than a shelf full of "how-to" books could ever have done.

12–117

COMMITMENT

1 John 2:15-17

(POSB, Note 1)

Remaining True to Your Word

When you gave your heart to Jesus, you made a specific promise to Him: not to love anyone or anything more than you love Him. Here is the story of one man who kept his promise.

One day, President Abraham Lincoln was riding in a coach with a colonel from Kentucky. The colonel took a bottle of whiskey out of his pocket. He offered Mr. Lincoln a drink. Mr. Lincoln said, "No thank you, Colonel. I never drink whiskey." In a little while, the colonel took some cigars out of his pocket and offered one to Mr. Lincoln. Again Mr. Lincoln said, "No, thank you, Colonel." Then Mr. Lincoln said, "I want to tell you a story."

"One day, when I was about nine years old, my mother called me to her bed. She was very sick. She said, 'Abe, the doctor tells me that I am not going to get well. I want you to be a good boy. I want you to promise me before I go that you will never use whiskey or tobacco as long as you live.' I promised my mother that I never would, and up to this hour, I kept this promise! Would you advise me to break that promise?"

The colonel put his hand on Mr. Lincoln's shoulder and said, "Mr. Lincoln, I would not have you break that promise for the world! It is one of the best promises you ever made. I would give a thousand dollars today if I had made my mother a promise like that and had kept it like you have done. I would be a much better man than I am!"[14]

Keep your promises to God. A compromise with the world can never be taken back.

12–118

COMMUNICATION

1 Peter 3:7

(POSB, Note 2)

Understanding Your Spouse

A husband cannot expect God to deposit information about his wife into his mind. The husband is charged to honor his wife. And he cannot do so without working to understand her. This fact is well illustrated by the lives of John and Jane.

"I don't want to talk about it any more! You just don't understand me." And for the "umpteenth" time, the chasm between John and Jane split into an even wider gap. Jane did not understand why John could not communicate better. Meanwhile, John was at a loss about what to do. The problem they faced is common to many married couples: two languages are being spoken and neither one can understand the other.

It was very ironic. John was known in his church as a great communicator, but he could not duplicate this same skill at home where it counted the most. On one particular day, he got fed up and asked the Lord what to do. During his prayer time, it suddenly dawned on him that he was able to communicate at church because he always *studied* his materials before he spoke.

Refreshed by this challenge, he began to devour books on the issues that affect Christian marriages. As he read, he realized he had never learned to listen to Jane. He knew a lot about her, but he really did not know her. He also discovered that learning *how* to say something to his wife was just as important as what he said. John decided to find out what she, as a woman, needed from him.

---

14 *Martin M. Hyzer.* Paul Lee Tan. *Encyclopedia of 7,700 Illustrations: Signs of the Times.* (Dallas, TX: Bible Communications, 1985), p.127.

> When John made Jane his focus of study, he was amazed how quickly he began to understand her. Jane noticed it too, and began to share her feelings more readily. The more John listened, the more he understood, and the more Jane willingly trusted him.

Where there is a desire to understand, communication is not far away. And where there is communication, trust and more understanding follow.

12–119

CONSCIENCE

1 Peter 3:13-17

(POSB, Note 4, point 2)

God Is Watching

To keep a clear conscience, your conduct must be suitable before men and God, as this story reminds us.

> A man went to steal corn from his neighbor's field. He took his little boy with him to keep a lookout, so as to give warning in case anyone should come along. Before commencing he looked all around, first one way and then the other. Not seeing any person, he was just about to fill his bag, when his son cried out, "Father, there is one way you haven't looked yet!" The father supposed that someone was coming, and asked his son which way he meant. He answered, "You forgot to look up!" The father, conscience-stricken, took his boy by the hand, and hurried home without the corn...he had [planned] to take.[15]

If you fail to look up, you'd better look out! Remember, God is watching.

12–120

CONVICTION

1 Peter 2:11-12

(POSB, Note 1, point 2)

Being Heavenly-Minded

As you journey through this life, where are you establishing roots? Are you getting comfortable here on earth? Is the here and now becoming your true home? Or does heaven tug at the strings of your heart? Listen to the account of one woman who had heaven on her mind.

> Several years ago a Christian woman told...about an incident with a young man who had been asking to date her. He was not a member of the church, and they just didn't have anything in common. She had turned him down twice and now she had said "no" to attending a rock concert with him. In a kind of mock exasperation, the young man asked, "What do you do for fun? You don't dance, you don't drink, you don't attend rock concerts, what do you do for fun?"
>
> To the young man she replied, "For fun I get up in the morning without feeling embarrassed, ashamed and guilty about what I did the night before."

15 *Prairie Overcomer.* Walter B. Knight. *Knight's Master Book of 4,000 Illustrations*, p.102.

The young man had nothing more to say. She was right; it *is* fun not to feel guilty for your actions the night before.

Come to think of it, there are many things in life that are fun. For example, that Christian girl is now married to a fine Christian man. They have a little girl and are building an outstanding Christian home together....She is having fun every day living without the affliction of deep scars of fornication, drugs or alcohol, and regrets from her past. It's fun getting ready each afternoon to receive a husband home from work, knowing that he won't be stopping off at a local bar for a few drinks with the boys. It is fun knowing that while he is away from her, his Christian conduct won't allow infidelity or even flirting. It's fun watching him hold his little girl on his lap with his loving, protecting arms. It's fun knowing that her little girl will never see her father in a drunken stupor or experimenting with drugs. It's fun living with assurance that the home will be led by a spiritual leader who will guide each family member toward heaven.

The list of fun things for Christians is endless; what do you do for fun?[16]

The best way to keep heaven in mind is to keep worldliness out of your heart.

12–121

CONVICTION

1 Peter 4:1-6

(POSB, Note 4)

Living What You Believe

The world cannot understand a Christian believer's convictions. The believer's drive is to please the Lord—as the world looks on and wonders what to think.

Donald Barnhouse gives us an example of a man who refused to compromise his spiritual convictions.

> In the summer of 1924 the young Scot, Eric Liddell, faced two great moments of his life: As a student of the ministry he was soon to be ordained; as an aspiring sprinter he was favored to bring glory to England by winning the 100-meter dash at the Olympic games in Paris.
>
> When Liddell discovered that this event was scheduled for a Sunday afternoon, it was a crucial moment for him; he believed that it was not to the glory of God for him to compete on Sunday. [Although he had only been trained to run the 100-meter dash, Liddell changed his plans and entered a different race, scheduled for a day other than Sunday.]
>
> [Thereafter], the young Scot made one major change in his daily round of study and athletic practice; he dropped his customary nightly discussion with his classmates. After the evening meal he left the dining hall, disappeared, and returned to his room hours later, tired and spent. His friends were perplexed, but he never told them where he went.
>
> The whole world learned his secret, at the Olympics. Eric Liddell, received the Gold Medal as 400-meter champion.

---

16 Ted Kyle and John Todd. *A Treasury of Bible Illustrations*, pp.58-59.

PRACTICAL ILLUSTRATIONS

> Eric Liddell not only made a record for speed in the 400-meter class; he made a record of God's work in a man's heart, and a testimony to faithfulness. Eric Liddell was faithful in one thing, and the Lord honored him in another.[17]

The world looks at conviction and says, "How strange!" God looks at conviction and says, "How strong!"

12–122

DECEPTION

2 John 7-13

(POSB, Note 1, point 1)

Beware of Deceivers

The mission of a deceiver is simple: to deceive. Every believer should be grounded in the truth in order to ward off the evil advances of those who distort the truth. A deceiver is an agent of Satan. Because Satan is the father of lies, do not trust anything his disciples say to you.

> A young man...stood on the outside of a crowd and boasted that he would make the...[street-corner] preacher...[quit] preaching. He shouted: "Hi, Mister, you can go home; you needn't preach any more—the Devil's dead!"
>
> The preacher looked at the young man sternly, and replied: "The Devil's dead? Then you're an orphan!"[18]

12–123

DECEPTION

2 John 7-13

(POSB, Note 2)

Guard Your Reward

The believer is strongly warned never to rest on his accolades nor to become passive toward the truth.

> There is the story told of a city slicker who decided to become a farmer. He bought a farm and moved his family out to the country. The man who sold the farm to him had said, "Mister, it's pretty simple out here: till the soil, plant the seed, pull the weeds, pray for rain, and then harvest the crop."
>
> The city slicker had gotten a good deal on the farm, and it was a first-rate farm with plenty of rich soil and excellent irrigation. By harvest time the city slicker felt he would be known as a skilled farmer. But this is not the end of the story.
>
> During the growing season, the city slicker saved on labor costs by not pulling the weeds. He reasoned the crops would grow faster than the weeds and smother out whatever weeds shot up. But when harvest time came, he was in for a rude awakening. What should have been a bumper crop turned out to be a catastrophic failure.

---

17 Donald Grey Barnhouse. *Let Me Illustrate.* (Grand Rapids, MI: Fleming H. Revell, 1967), p.85.

18 *Christian Herald.* Walter B. Knight. *3,000 Illustrations for Christian Service*, p.233.

The city slicker had been given the opportunity of a lifetime, but he lost it all because he allowed the weeds to choke out the crops. He lost his reward. In the same sense, the Christian believer can have a field of blessings in store. But if false teaching is allowed to take over, it can ruin everything he or she has ever worked for.

You've come too far to turn back now—keep on weeding out the lies and deception! Remember, harvest time *is coming*.

12–124

DISCIPLESHIP

2 John 1-4

Leading Others to Walk in Truth

(POSB, Note 4)

Do your children, either physical or spiritual children, walk in the truth? If so, it is one of the greatest testimonies for you as a Christian believer. There is no better use of your time than to invest in the lives of others.

A college student and part-time youth leader met an eleven-year old boy during a summer church retreat. The eleven-year old's sincere love for Christ was easily noticed. The youth leader soon invited the young boy to travel with the youth team to share his testimony with other kids.

As the eleven-year old grew in age, he also grew in his walk with Christ. The young college student eventually married and moved away. But years later the former youth worker received a touching letter from the boy he had once discipled. Now a young man himself, he wrote a letter of thanks to his onetime mentor. A portion of the letter read:

"I'm not sure if you realize the impact you had on my life, but I am now a pastor. As I look back at my Christian journey, I cannot think of anyone who gave me more opportunities for ministry than you. No one else dared to believe in me. Thanks for being my teacher. It was a privilege being your student. I grew more under the influence of your ministry than any other time in my life. Thank you!"

The youth worker put down the letter. Tears of joy made any further reading impossible. The young boy had become an adult, was still walking in the truth, and was now influencing others to do the same.

What a legacy! There is a bumper sticker that reads, "Have you hugged your child today?" For the purpose of this point, believers should ask themselves daily, "Have you inspired your kids to walk in truth today?"

12–125

ETERNAL LIFE

1 Peter 3:10-12

God Is the Source

(POSB, Note 4, point 2)

Man is able to love and enjoy life because God has given it to him. This story, from the pages of American history, frames this point for us.

Once when Calvin Coolidge was Vice President and presiding over the Senate, an altercation arose between two Senators. Tempers flared, and one Senator told the other to go straight to hell. The offended Senator stormed from his seat, marched down the aisle and stood before Mr. Coolidge, who was silently leafing through a book.

"Mr. [Vice] President," he said, "did you hear what he said to me?"

Coolidge looked up from his book and said calmly, "You know, I have been looking through the rule book. You don't have to go."[19]

Remember, God, not man, is the source of eternal life. It is up to you to choose the right path.

12–126

EVANGELISM

1 John 5:6-8

We Have a Mission

(POSB, Note 1, point 1)

Jesus Christ, God's only Son, is our great Example. He never missed an opportunity to fulfill His mission—to seek and save the lost. Note the stirring words of D.L. Moody:

> If the ministers would encourage their members to be scattered among the audience, to never mind their pews, but sit where they can watch the faces of the audience, it would be a good thing. In Scotland, I met a man who with his wife would sit, and they said, so as to watch for souls. When they saw any one who seemed impressed, they would go to those persons after the meting and talk with them. Nearly all the conversions in that church during the last fifteen months had been made through that influence.
>
> Now, if we could only have...members of the church whose business it is just to watch, and...afterwards clinch them in. The best way in our regular churches is to let the workers all help pull the net in. You will get a good many fishes; it won't be now and then one, but scores and scores.[20]

Christ fulfilled His mission, giving His life on the cross to pay the terrible debt of man's sin. Our mission is to tell others—to seek out the lost wherever they may be and tell them there *is* a Savior.

12–127

FAITH

1 John 5:1-5

The Power to Overcome

(POSB, Note 3)

Are you overcoming the world—or are you being overcome by the world? There is no mistaking the fact that believers are really warriors in a world that is out to destroy them. Imagine, if you will, a Christian warrior in the heat of battle.

19 *Lester Buford.* Paul Lee Tan. *Encyclopedia of 7,700 Illustrations: Signs of the Times*, p.690.

20 John W. Reed, Editor. *1100 Illustrations from the Writings of D. L. Moody.* (Grand Rapids, MI: Baker Books, 1996), p. 89.

The setting is in the believer's home ... the believer is in his or her comfortable chair ... holding the television's remote control and flipping from channel to channel. As the individual flips through the channels, the enemy soon appears:

⇒ On channel one profanity abounds and God's name is cursed.
⇒ On another channel you see more skin than clothes.
⇒ On one more channel morality is mocked as if it were a vice, a sin.
⇒ On yet another channel—well, you do not want to know.

On and on the list could go. The Christian believer begins to reel from the blows of the world. He is ever so close to giving up and giving in. He is drowning in the sewage-filled waves. How can he save himself from this situation? What turns the tide during the believer's battle with the world? Faith and only faith will scatter the enemy.

With a mighty sweep of his hand, the Christian warrior presses the "off" button and thwarts another effort by the world to drag him down. Overcoming faith is *believing* that God is in control and then *acting* on it!

"I will set no worthless thing before my eyes..." (Ps.101:3, NASB).

12–128

FALSE TEACHERS
1 John 2:18-23
(POSB, Note 2)

Beware False Teachers Within the Church

Many people expect antichrists and false teachers to come from a cult or some wildly fanatic religious group. But that is not always the case. False teachers often come from within the church. That's right—the church... from any church. If *you* were the enemy, wouldn't you place your terrorists behind the enemy's lines?

Ken was a Sunday School teacher at a large church. The church was at one time very conservative. Members had grown up believing that the Bible was the Word of God—from cover to cover. But over time, like too many churches, the focus had shifted away from Christ and the authority of the Scriptures. Eventually, all kinds of teaching found its way into the classrooms and pulpit.

Ken was the product of a system that had shifted its focus from God's Word to "self-help" programs. He taught from sources other than the Bible, sources that did not have lasting power to change the problems of men.

Not long into Ken's teaching term, Satan began to open fire on the class. Ken became frustrated. People were not changing for good. In fact, some were slipping further away from God and from the church. One Sunday, after another "flat" lesson, he vented his feelings to a fellow teacher. "I don't get it. I teach my heart out every Sunday and all I get is blank stares."

In as gentle a way as possible, his associate replied: "Ken, what do you expect? You don't teach from the Bible, our ultimate authority and guide, so how can you expect your students to believe it and be changed by it?" You are teaching *man's* word, not God's Word.

Make sure *you* are being taught the truth of God's Word—no matter who the teacher is.

12–129

FALSE TEACHERS
Jude 3-16
(POSB, Note 8, point 2)

The Consequences of Deception

What is a false teacher? Simply this: someone who proclaims lies as if they were the truth. Who will be judged for teaching what is false? Any who do so. Carefully consider the following account:

A melon farmer's crop of melons was disappearing fast from his field. Thieves were continually stealing the melons under the cover of night's darkness. The farmer finally became desperate and in an attempt to save his crop from the vandals he decided to put up a sign.

The sign had on it a skull and crossbones, and it read: "ONE OF THESE MELONS IS POISONED"—only the farmer knew that it was not true.

Sure enough, for two nights not a melon was missing. But, after the third night, the farmer noticed that his sign had been altered. Someone had scratched out the word "ONE" and replaced it with another word so that the sign now read: "TWO OF THESE MELONS ARE POISONED."

Thinking to save his whole crop through deception, he lost it all, which just goes to illustrate Sir Walter Scott's observation:

Oh, what a tangled web we weave,
When we practice to deceive![21]

Only by knowing the truth will you be protected from the lies of the false teacher.

12–130

FALSE TEACHERS
Jude 3-16
(POSB, Note 15)

Empty Promises Leading Nowhere

Be careful who you turn to when you need direction. There are many false teachers in the world offering something that resembles hope. But you will be very lost if you place your trust in them. False teachers cannot even discern where they are going. But it certainly isn't heaven.

In the Disney animated classic *Alice in Wonderland,* Alice wanders through a frustrating world of tardy rabbits, singing flowers, and one curious-talking cat. Her visit with the cat begins as she continues down a mysterious darkened trail and stops at a large tree. The tree is covered with signs that point in every possible direction: "Up," "Down," "Yonder," "Back," "This Way," and "That Way." Poor Alice looks more confused than ever and asks herself, "Now let's see. Where was I? I wonder which way I ought to go?"

21 Michael P. Green. *Illustrations for Biblical Preaching,* p.229.

Just then, Alice hears a melodic voice that seems to be drifting down from the trees. She looks all around and finally observes two ghostly eyes and a wide toothy grin floating amongst the boughs of the great tree.

The grinning teeth inquire of Alice, "Lose something?"

"N-n-no, I was just..." stammers Alice in reply.

Suddenly, a pink striped feline body emerges from the branches.

"Oh, you're a cat!"

"A Cheshire cat," he responds.

"I just want to ask which way I ought to go," asks Alice.

"Well that depends on where you want to get to," says the cat.

"Well, it really doesn't matter," answers Alice.

"Then it really doesn't matter which way you go," says the enigmatic cat just before vanishing into the woods again.[22]

The Cheshire cat is the perfect picture of a false teacher. He pretends to be knowledgeable and able to offer help. But when it comes to pointing you in the right direction, his promise of hope quickly disappears.

12–131

FALSE TEACHERS

2 Peter 2:1-9

(POSB, Note 1)

Heed the Warning Signs

How well do you listen when someone is teaching from the Bible? Each believer has a responsibility to discern what is being said. When you least expect it, a false teacher could be hard at work, sowing his seeds of lurking, just waiting to deceive you and destroy your faith.

Every year, thousands upon thousands of wildebeests run a marathon of amazing proportions. The African savannah has been dry for weeks. Now, rains have come to the north. Small herds of wildebeests join other herds of the hog-like creatures as they run for days. Covering many miles at a thundering speed, the larger herds grows to an unbelievable two million.

Driven by instinct, the wildebeest perform their yearly ritual, running at full speed. Then, all at once, they come to an orchestrated stop. There, at the edge of a particular river, they sense danger in the air. Baboons in the trees overhead watch with great anticipation, knowing what is going to happen next.

A few wildebeests venture to the edge of the river. The water is so inviting after the dry season and after their long, long journey. Oh, to take from the cool water. The feeling of danger is intense, but so is their desire for the refreshing water.

Eventually, a few dare to drink, watching ever so carefully. But the danger is not visible. The few wildebeests that ignore their feelings of danger and begin to drink are at once taken in by the cool refreshing river water. They drink more heartily.

Then, in one swift action, large hungry crocodiles emerge from beneath the river. They grab their victims in their powerful jaws and yank them into the water. The wildebeests are torn limb from limb, but only because the famished crocodiles cannot

22 *Alice in Wonderland* (Walt Disney, 1951), directed by Hamilton Luske and Clyde Geronimi. As quoted in PreachingToday.com

swallow them whole. The baboons swoon and howl, but the declaration of impending doom is all too late. What had briefly seemed a refreshing source of life-giving water quickly turned into a deceptive death-trap.

We must heed the danger signs given in Scripture. Do not be taken in by the tricks of false teachers. Test all teaching and preaching by the Word of God!

12–132

FALSE TEACHERS

2 Peter 2:10-22

(POSB, Note 8)

Keeping Your Guard Up

By definition, a false teacher's life is void of truth. In an attempt to be received by believers, these deceivers will mask themselves with false spirituality. Author and Pastor Warren Wiersbe illuminates this point with a personal story.

In one of the churches I pastored, I noticed that a young man in the choir was doing his utmost to appear a "spiritual giant" to the other choir members, especially the younger women. He prayed with fervency and often talked about his walk with the Lord. Some of the people were impressed by him, but I felt that something was wrong and that danger was in the air.

Sure enough, he began to date one of the fine young ladies who happened to be a new believer. In spite of my warnings, she continued the friendship, which ended in her being seduced. I praise God that she was rescued and is now faithfully serving God, but she could have avoided that terrible experience.[23]

The surest way to stay out of the wolf-trap is to stay in the sheep-fold—to be firmly grounded in the Word of God.

12–133

FALSE TEACHERS

Jude 3-10

(POSB, Note 2)

Prepare to Face the Enemy

It is Satan's plan to infiltrate the church of Jesus Christ with false teachers whenever and wherever he can.

A Christian minister once had a member of a well-known Jehovah's Witness cult in his audience who constantly interrupted the meeting by shouting and heckling. "You cannot prove that Jesus is the eternal Son of God," he said. "He was the FIRSTBORN of every creature; so He could not be deity. The eternal Father must therefore be older than His Son; and if Christ is not as old as His father, then HE is not eternal, if HE is not eternal, HE cannot be God."

The preacher carefully considered the statement, "A father must be older than his son"; then he [gave] this withering reply: "While you might make such a point

23 Warren W. Wiersbe. *The Bible Exposition Commentary, Vol.2.* (Wheaton, IL: Victor Books, 1989), p.454.

concerning an earthly parent, it certainly does not apply when we speak of God. I will prove that [to] you by your own words.

"You have just called God the eternal Father. But how can God be the eternal FATHER (not just God) without having an eternal Son? Eternal FATHERHOOD demands eternal SONSHIP! When did your own paternal parent begin to be your father? At the very moment you became his son, and not before! While time must elapse before one can become a human father, this is not true of God. He is the eternal Father, and therefore He must have an eternal Son!" The critic fell silent as he pondered the preacher's words.[24]

Since false teachers will creep into the church, the best way to protect yourself is to study the truth about Jesus Christ and the truths of God's Word. If you are faithful in the study of God's Holy Word, He will protect you from error.

12–134

FALSE TEACHERS

2 Peter 2:1-9

(POSB, Note 4)

Warning: Avoid Self-Exaltation

The Scripture is unmistakably clear: Christian believers are never to exploit others for their own gain. The work we do is to be for the advancement of the kingdom of God, for the good of all believers, as the following bit of history so well illustrates.

Everybody knows of Isaac Newton's famed encounter with a falling apple, and how Newton introduced the laws of gravity and revolutionized astronomical studies. But few know that if it weren't for Edmund Halley, the world may never have heard of Newton. Halley was the one who challenged Newton to think through his original theories. He corrected Newton's mathematical errors and prepared geometrical figures to support his discovers. It was Halley who coaxed the hesitant Newton to write his great work, Mathematical Principles of Natural Philosophy. And it was Halley who edited and supervised its publication, financing its printing even though Newton was wealthier and could better afford the cost.

Historians have called Halley's relationship with Newton one of the most selfless examples in science. Newton began almost immediately to reap the rewards of prominence; Halley received little credit. He did use the principles Newton developed to predict the orbit and return of a comet that would later bear his name, but since Halley's Comet only returns every 76 years, few hear his name. Still, Halley didn't care who received credit as long as the cause of science was advanced. HE was content to live without fame.

Sometimes just the reward of what we are doing far outweighs the recognition we often think we need to have.[25]

---

24 Paul Lee Tan. *Encyclopedia of 15,000 Illustrations.* (Dallas, TX: Bible Communications, Inc., 1998), #6070.

25 *God's Little Devotional Book.* (Tulsa, OK: Honor Books, Inc., 1995), p.107.

12–135

FALSE TEACHING

2 John 7-13

(POSB, Note 4)

Truth—the Safeguard Against Cults

Would you allow an enemy into your home whose mission was to destroy you? Of course not. But every day members of cults are invited into the homes of many who know no better. If the devil's agents come knocking on your door, will you let them in?

> One day two members of a cult knocked on the door of a suburban home. They had their speech all prepared, a speech geared to gain them converts.
>
> The owner of the home opened the door and greeted them. "Hi there. We're having a Bible study. Do you want to join us?" The two cult members knew they were out of their comfort zone when they peered inside and noticed a number of people with Bibles in their laps.
>
> The cult members politely backed up then sped for safety. After going a few blocks, the younger cult member asked his mentor why they had left so quickly. The older member said, "We've been trained to teach them what we *think*, not to listen to what they *know*. Those people, not us, would have been in control. From now on, let's be sure we avoid doors with those fish symbols. We need to look elsewhere!"

Do cult members ever knock at your door? God's Word is clear: Send them quickly on their way. Let God's Word be your protection.

12–136

FALSE TEACHING

1 John 4:1-6

(POSB, Note 1)

Trying the Spirits

Carlos Santana recently won eight Grammy awards for his album *Supernatural,* which has sold more than 10 million copies. A recent *Rolling Stone* profile of Santana describes Santana's spirituality:

> His meditation spot is in front of the fireplace.... A card with the word Metatron is spelled out in intricately painted picture letters lies on the floor next to the fireplace. Metatron is an angel. Santana has been in regular contact with him since 1994. Carlos will sit here facing the wall, the candles lit. He has a yellow legal pad at one side, ready for the communications that will come. "It's kind of like a fax machine," he says....
>
> There are few conversations with [Santana] that don't lead to discussion of angels, or of the spiritual radio through which music comes. Santana has been increasingly engaged by angels since the day in 1988 when he picked up a book on the subject at the Milwaukee airport. "It's an enormous peace, the few times I have felt the presence in the room," he says....
>
> "My reality is that God speaks to you every day. There's an inner voice, and when you hear it, you get a little tingle in your medulla oblongata at the back of your neck, a little shiver, and at two o'clock in the morning, everything's really quiet and you meditate and you got the candles, you got the incense and you've been chanting, and all of

a sudden you hear this voice: Write this down. It is just an inner voice, and you trust it. That voice will never take you to the desert...."

Santana credits Metatron with alerting him to the recent changes in his life.[26]

Sounds enlightening, doesn't it? Of course, it is nothing short of communicating with demons, which the Bible strictly warns us against. We must apply the Word of God, testing the spirits of all who claim to give good guidance. If a person doesn't line up with the Scripture, do not follow him. Be sure, absolutely sure, that the teacher you follow is of God.

12–137

FELLOWSHIP

1 John 1:1-5

(POSB, Note 4, point 1)

The Loving Reach of God

Christian fellowship is one of the greatest blessings of being a child of God. Imagine how rich you are: You have the opportunity to have intimate fellowship with God the Father, your Creator, with God the Son, your Savior, with the Holy Spirit, God's abiding presence within you, as well as with other believers. The following poem expresses the thought well.

Jesus understood
The loving reach of God
The longing reach of men
In his life, in his death
He joined their hands together
—Anonymous

Are you taking full advantage of the fellowship God has made available to you with Himself and with other believers? If not, you are robbing yourself of joy beyond measure!

12–138

FLATTERY

Jude 3-16

(POSB, Note 22)

Words Without Sincerity

A false teacher is quick to flatter and exalt people for his own gain. But once he has exploited a person, the deceiver's flowery words quickly change to expose his true heart.

Some time ago, the Saturday Evening Post ran a humorous article that traced the tendency for marriage partners to drift from a height of bliss into the humdrum of

---

26 *Santana's Wayward Spirituality*. Preaching Today.com. *Citation*: Chris Heath, "The Epic Life of Carlos Santana," *Rolling Stone* (4-16-00), p.41.

routine attitudes. Called "The Seven Ages of the Married Cold," the article likens the state of the marriage to the reaction of a husband to his wife's colds during seven years of marriage.

The first year: "Sugar dumpling, I'm worried about my baby girl. You've got a bad sniffle and there's no telling about these things with all this strep around. I'm putting you in the hospital this afternoon for a general checkup and a good rest. I know the food's lousy, but I'll bring your meals from Rossini's. I've already got it arranged with the floor superintendent."

The second year: "Listen darling, I don't like the sound of that cough and I've called Doc Miller to rush over here. Now you go to bed like a good girl, please? Just for Papa."

The third year: "Maybe you'd better lie down, honey; nothing like having a little rest when you feel punk. I'll bring you something to eat. Have we got any soup?"

The fourth year: "Look dear, be sensible. After you feed the kids and get the dishes washed, you'd better hit the sack."

The fifth year: "Why don't you get yourself a couple of aspirin?"

The sixth year: "If you'd just gargle or something, instead of sitting around barking like a seal!"

The seventh year: "For Pete's sake, stop sneezing! Whatcha trying to do, gimme pneumonia?"[27]

Whether false teacher or solid Christian, your words matter—they will eventually reveal your true feelings. Be sure your compliments are truly heartfelt, not empty flattery for your own gain.

12–139

FORGIVENESS

1 John 1:6-7

(POSB, Note 2, point 2)

Clean on the Inside

Little children have a unique way of capturing the truth of God's Word in ways that often escape adults. This is one little girl's interpretation of John 3:16.

[Dr. Walter Wilson] was visiting in a home and the members of the family were asked to quote Bible verses.

One little girl quoted John 3:16 as follows: "For God so loved the world, that He gave His only begotten Son, so that whosoever believeth in Him, should not perish but have INTERNAL LIFE."[28]

The point is well stated: if you walk in the light of Christ, His blood will cleanse you from the inside out. Thank God for INTERNAL LIFE!

27 Michael P. Green. *Illustrations for Biblical Preaching*, pp.233-234.

28 Paul Lee Tan. *Encyclopedia of 7,700 Illustrations: Signs of the Times*, p.441.

12–140

GODLINESS

1 John 3:1-3

(POSB, Note 3)

The Secret to Holiness

Living a pure life takes total commitment. Therefore, we must be very careful: what we hold on to will also hold on to us.

> Just out of reach from my window stretches a wire which carries a heavy current of electricity for light and power. It is carefully insulated at every pole that supports it, and it is carried well out of common reach....Yet the doves light on it and take no harm....The secret is that when they touch the full-powered wire they touch nothing else. The give themselves wholly to it.
>
> My danger would be that while I touched the wire I should also be touching the earth through the walls of my house, and the current would turn my body into a channel for escape. But they [the doves] rest wholly on the wire and experience neither dread nor danger. They are one with it, and they are safe.
>
> So would God have us seek our safety in complete self-surrender to His power and love. It is when we reach one hand to Him, while yet we keep fast hold on some forbidden thing with the other, that we are in danger.[29]

Are you holding on to something that is forbidden? It's time to let go and let God take over!

12–141

GOSPEL

1 John 2:24-27

(POSB, Note 1)

Abiding in Christ—a Way of Life

Does the gospel abide in you? Or does it come and go according to your circumstances, with compromise replacing conviction? The reality of the gospel can be confirmed in your life when it propels you to remain consistent. This example makes a good point.

> The following is a Russian parable. A hunter raised his rifle and took careful aim at a large bear. When about to pull the trigger, the bear spoke in a soft, soothing voice, "Isn't it better to talk than to shoot? What do you want? Let us negotiate the matter."
>
> Lowering his rifle, the hunter replied, "I want a fur coat." "Good," said the bear, "that is a negotiable question. I only want a full stomach, so let us negotiate a compromise."
>
> They sat down to negotiate, and after a time the bear walked away *alone*. The negotiations had been successful. The bear had a full stomach, and the hunter had his fur coat. [But not in the way he expected it!] Compromises rarely satisfy both sides in equal measure.[30]

Never compromise with the enemy. You will lose every time. Keep abiding in the Word and in Christ. It is the only way to be safe!

29 Isaac Rankin, in *The Friend.* Walter B. Knight. *3,000 Illustrations for Christian Service*, p.172.

30 Michael P. Green. *Illustrations for Biblical Preaching*, p.76.

12–142

GRACE

1 Peter 1:10-12

(POSB, Note 2)

The Great Mercy of God

How merciful our great God is! While we deserve the severest judgment, He has instead offered us His grace.

Oppressed by the noonday heat, a tired farmer sat under a walnut tree to rest. Relaxing, he looked at his pumpkin vines and said to himself, "How strange it is that God puts such big heavy pumpkins on a frail vine that has so little strength it has to trail on the ground!"

And then looking up into the cool branches of the tree above him, he added, "How strange it is that God puts small walnuts on such a big tree with branches so strong they could hold a man!"

Just then a breeze dislodged a walnut from the tree. The tired farmer wondered no more, as he rubbed his head ruefully and said, "It is a good thing there wasn't a pumpkin up there instead of a walnut."—SOURCE UNKNOWN

And it is a good thing for believers that eternal mercy and grace awaits us, as we cannot imagine what life would be like if God gave us what we *really* deserved.

12–143

GRACE

2 Peter 3:15-18

(POSB, Note 3)

Sharing the Good News

We need to give Jesus Christ all the praise for our salvation. Just think: those who love Him will live with Him forever! Author Max Lucado gives us special insight into the grace of God.

A fellow is doing some shopping at a commissary on a military base. Doesn't need much, just some coffee and a loaf of bread. He is standing in line at the checkout stand. Behind him is a woman with a full cart. Her basket overflows with groceries, clothing, and a VCR.

At his turn he steps up to the register. The clerk invites him to draw a piece of paper out of a fishbowl. "If you pull out the correct slip, then all your groceries are free," the clerk explains.

"How many 'correct slips' are there?" asks the buyer.

"Only one."

The bowl is full so the chances are slim, but the fellow tries anyway, and wouldn't you know it, he gets the winning ticket! What a surprise. But then he realizes he is only buying coffee and bread. What a waste.

But this fellow is quick. He turns to the lady behind him—the one with the mountain of stuff—and proclaims, "Well, what do you know, Honey? We won! We don't have to pay a penny."

She stares at him. He winks at her. And somehow she has the wherewithal to play along. She steps up beside him. Puts her arm in his and smiles. And for a moment they stand side-by-side, wedded by good fortune. In the parking lot she consummates the temporary union with a kiss and a hug and goes her way with a grand story to tell her friends.

I know, I know. What they did was a bit shady. He shouldn't have lied and she shouldn't have pretended. But that taken into account, it's still a nice story.

A story not too distant from our own. We, too, have been graced with a surprise. Even more than that of the lady. For though her debt was high, she could pay it. We can't begin to pay ours.

We, like the woman, have been given a gift. Not just at the checkout stand, but at the judgment seat.

And we, too, have become a bride. Not just for a moment, but for eternity. And not just for groceries, but for the feast. Don't we have a grand story to tell our friends?[31]

Praise God, we do have a grand story to tell! Who will you share it with today?

12–144

GROWTH, CHRISTIAN

Jude 1-2

Keep Pressing On

(POSB, Note 2, point 4)

As a Christian, do you think you have finally arrived? That you are as good as you can be? Think again. On one hand, you made a start when you accepted Jesus Christ as your Savior. But on the other hand, you have a long way to go. Although Jesus Christ has accepted you just as you are, it does not mean you can just sit back and do nothing. Listen to this striking story.

Many years ago, a promising Greek artist named Timanthes was under the instruction of a well-known tutor. After several years, the young painter created an exquisite portrait. He was so thrilled with what he had painted that he sat day after day gazing at his work.

One morning, however, he was horrified to discover that his teacher had deliberately ruined his painting. Angry and in tears, Timanthes ran to him and asked why he had destroyed his cherished possession. The wise man replied, "I did it for your own good. That painting was retarding your progress. It was an excellent piece of art, but it was not perfect. Start again and see if you can do even better." The student took his advice and produced a master-piece called "Sacrifice of Iphigenia," regarded by some as one of the finest paintings of antiquity.

God never wants us to be content with our accomplishments. He wants us to reach even higher plateaus of service and Christlikeness...Child of God, don't be satisfied with your spiritual attainments. With His help, keep pressing on![32]

As a believer, you must never be satisfied; you must continue to press on toward perfection.

---

31 Max Lucado. *When God Whispers Your Name.* (Dallas, TX: Word Publishing, 1994), pp.71-72.

32 Craig B. Larson, Editor. *Illustrations for Preaching & Teaching*, p.206.

12–145

HEAVEN

1 Peter 1:1-2

(POSB, Note 1)

The Believer's Eternal Home

All across the world are millions of refugees. Forced into a new and often harsh way of life by war, politics, economics, and natural disasters, these people have no home to call their own. Here is one such story.

"We cannot stay here any longer," Louis said, resigning himself to take his wife and two children away from a deserted bus. It had been a place of shelter for over a year but, due to rust, leaks in the roof drove them to seek a dryer refuge. "Where can we go?" he wondered. Louis had lost his job and could not afford even the cheapest apartment in town. Food was scarce. Someone was always sick with a cold. All his years spent in training seemed to be wasted. "Whatever happened to the dream I was pursuing?" Louis wondered, as he reviewed in his mind how hard life had gotten.

At one time in Louis' life, he would have been considered successful even by worldly standards. But through a series of unfortunate circumstances, he found himself homeless and on the streets. Eventually, he was able to find a job to support his family. Soon after, the Lord provided a home for them. Through the process of his pain, Louis learned a lot about what is important in life. One of the striking lessons Louis learned was that the things of this earth are temporary, fleeting. Heaven was his real and eternal home. In this life, he was simply passing through.

Are you heaven-bound?

12–146

HOLY–HOLINESS

1 Peter 1:13-16

(POSB, Note 3, point 3)

Staying Pure in an Impure World

God has called you to a life of holiness. But how? How can you be holy when you live in an unholy world?

A woman from Berne, Switzerland, tells us this story of her country's flower, the edelweiss. The very name of this plant is a story in itself. Edelweiss is a compound word which in the German means "noble and white." It is a small perennial herb of the aster family whose pure white blossom must be sought after, since it nestles in the highest snowy crags of the Alps. It is so absolutely white that it blends perfectly with its environment, losing its identifying characteristics completely in its surroundings.

Even when picked and pressed in paper for preservation, it remains free from discoloration for many years. If we would be like the edelweiss, we must keep ourselves pure and noble, striving to attain the heights with God. Then, as He keeps us pure in heart and motive, He will enable us to accept with humility the loss of our own status in the scope of His larger landscape.[33]

---

33 Spiros Zodhiates, Th.D. *Illustrations of Bible Truths.* (Chattanooga, TN: AMG International, 1995), p.191.

To remain pure and holy, you must be like the edelweiss, surrounding yourself with the things of God. Only then can He make you exactly what He desires you to be.

12–147

HOLY SPIRIT

1 John 2:24-27

(POSB, Note 4, point 3)

The Abiding Presence of God

What kind of relationship do you have with the Holy Spirit? Some people act as if He doesn't exist. Others fail to credit Him with being fully God. Still others are intimidated by those He fills with His power. There are even people who try to *control* the Holy Spirit. Despite all the misconceptions, the Holy Spirit has a very important role to play in the life of every believer.

> Benjamin West, the great painter, speaking of Gilbert Stuart, a brother artist famed for his beautiful coloring, used to say to his pupils, "It's no use to steal Stuart's colors; if you want to paint as he does, you must steal his eyes."
>
> When we are baffled in our efforts to live as Christ lived, the record of His life, however wonderful it is, will not enable us to be like Him. What we need is His heart, His nature. Only [His] divinity within us can recognize divinity without. Without the Holy Spirit, we cannot know Him as God.[34]

The Holy Spirit is your only hope of remaining in Christ. Do you give Him His proper place in your heart and life?

12–148

HOLY SPIRIT

1 John 3:18-24

(POSB, Note 5)

The Source of Abundant Life

What is the secret to an abundant Christian life? The secret is the Source—the Holy Spirit living in the hearts of believers. The overflowing Christian life is the Spirit-filled life: when there is more of *Him* in you than *you*. Ruby Miller shares this practical visual aid on the ministry of the Holy Spirit.

> Paul tells us to live victoriously and to avoid excesses of the flesh. [D.L.] Moody once illustrated this truth as follows: "Tell me," he said to his audience, "How can I get the air out this glass?" One man said, "Suck it out with a pump." Moody replied, "That would create a vacuum and shatter the glass."
>
> After many impossible suggestions, Moody smiled, picked up a pitcher of water, and filled the glass. "There," he said, "all the air is now removed." He then went on to

34 Spiros Zodhiates, Th.D. *Illustrations of Bible Truths*, p.120.

show that victory in the Christian life is not by "sucking out a sin here and there," but rather by being filled with the Spirit.[35]

More of Him…less of me…from sin, Holy Spirit, set me free.

12–149

HOPE

1 Peter 1:3-5

(POSB, Note 1, point 3)

The Ability to Keep Hope Alive

If you had been one of Jesus' first disciples, would you have lost hope after He was crucified? As you recall, all of Jesus' closest disciples hid themselves in a room, shaking with fear. Jesus' promise to rise from the dead had been pushed from their memories. It was only after the resurrection of Christ that their hope was ignited.

The story is told of a man and his young son who went on a skiing trip in the country of Turkey. Surprised by a sudden snow storm, they became lost in the wilderness. The father, a man who had been trained to survive the elements, was able to keep himself and his son alive as they looked for civilization.

Meanwhile, in the outside world, hope for the man and his son began to fade with each passing day. After a week had gone by, the search teams were called back. Hope had died. Shrouded in grief, the family held a memorial service that broke even the toughest heart.

The next day, however, brought a remarkable turn of events. Despite all odds, the man had found help. After receiving treatment for himself and his son, the lost skiers were reunited with their family again. What a glorious day!

In this story, the lost skiers were only thought to be dead; but they were, in fact, alive. Likewise, believers, when they depart this earth, are still truly alive—a miracle made possible only through our Lord Jesus Christ.

12–150

HOSPITALITY

1 Peter 4:7-11

(POSB, Note 4)

Entertaining vs. Hospitality

One of the pillars of Christianity is in the area of relationships. In order to build relationships that are meaningful, we must be willing to open up our lives and our homes, willing to have the Lord use us and our homes to enrich the lives of others. But there is also the need to understand the difference between entertaining people and having the gift of hospitality. Karen Mains reminds us of this great difference.

35 Paul Lee Tan. *Encyclopedia of 7,700 Illustrations: Signs of the Times*, p.555.

Entertaining says, "I want to impress you with my home, my clever decorating, my cooking." Hospitality, seeking to minister, says, "This home is a gift from my Master. I use it as He desires." Hospitality aims to serve.

Entertaining puts things before people. "As soon as I get the house finished, the living room decorated, my housecleaning done—then I will start inviting people." Hospitality puts people first. "No furniture—we'll even eat on the floor!" "The decorating may never get done—you come anyway." "The house is a mess—but you are friends—come home with us."

Entertaining subtly declares, *"This home is mine, an expression of my personality. Look, please, and admire."* Hospitality whispers, *"What is mine is yours."*[36]

Are you in the business of entertaining, or of opening up your home to nurture and to minister to others?

12–151

HUMILITY

1 Peter 5:5-7

(POSB, Note 3, point 3)

Giving Your Cares to the Lord

If you stumble on your journey to heaven, do you have the assurance that your loving Father will come to help you? God has given the trusting believer one of the greatest promises in the Bible:

"Casting all your care upon him; for he careth for you" (1 Pt.5:7).

Author Max Lucado shares this touching story of a father's willingness to care for his son.

[Jim Redmond's son] Derek, a twenty-six-year-old Briton, was favored to win the four-hundred-meter race in the 1992 Barcelona Olympics. Halfway into his semifinal heat, a fiery pain seared through his right leg. He crumpled to the track with a torn hamstring.

As the medical attendants were approaching, Redmond fought to his feet. "It was animal instinct," he would later say. He set out hopping, pushing away the coaches in a crazed attempt to finish the race.

When he reached the stretch, a big man pushed through the crowd. He was wearing a T-shirt that read "Have you hugged your child today?" and a hat that challenged, "Just Do It." The man was Jim Redmond, Derek's father.

"You don't have to do this," he told his weeping son.

"Yes, I do," Derek declared.

"Well, then," said Jim, "we're going to finish this together."

And they did. Jim wrapped Derek's arm around his shoulder and helped him hobble to the finish line. Fighting off security men, the son's head sometimes buried in the father's shoulder, they stayed in Derek's lane to the end.

The crowd clapped, then stood, then cheered, and then wept as the father and son finished the race.

---

36 Karen Mains. *Open Heart, Open Home,* (Elgin, Ill: David C. Cook Publishing Co., 1976).

What made the father do it? What made the father leave the stands to meet his son on the track? Was it the strength of his child? No, it was the pain of his child. His son was hurt and fighting to complete the race. So the father came to help him finish.

God does the same. Our prayers may be awkward. Our attempts may be feeble. But since the power of prayer is in the one who hears it and not the one who says it, our prayers do make a difference.[37]

All you have to do is be humble enough to turn your cares over to the Lord. God is more than able to take care of anything you cast His way.

12–152

HUMILITY

1 Peter 5:5-7

(POSB, Note 2, point 2)

Putting Aside Privileges

A dangerous attitude to assume is that a person's *position* or *title* relieves the individual from the duty of serving others. This story from the pages of American history speaks loudly.

A rider on horseback, many years ago, came across a squad of soldiers who were trying to move a heavy piece of timber. A corporal stood by, giving lordly orders to "heave." But the piece of timber was a trifle too heavy for the squad.

"Why don't you help them?" asked the quiet man on the horse, addressing the important corporal.

"Me? Why, I'm a corporal, sir!" Dismounting, the stranger carefully took his place with the soldiers.

"Now, all together, boys—heave!" he said. And the big piece of timber slid into place. The stranger mounted his horse and addressed the corporal.

"The next time you have a piece of timber for your men to handle, corporal, send for your commander-in-chief."

The horseman was George Washington.[38]

And Jesus said,

"Just as the Son of Man did not come to be served, but to serve, and to give His life a ransom for many" (Mt.20:28, NASB).

12–153

HUMILITY

1 Peter 3:8-9

(POSB, Note 5)

Putting Others First

Walking in humility is a most endearing quality, as told in this story.

There is a legend of a man so much beloved of the angels for his saintliness that they asked God to bestow upon him some new power. They were permitted to ask him

37 Max Lucado. *He Still Moves Stones.* (Dallas, TX: Word Publishing, 1993), pp.101-102.

38 *Watchman-Examiner.* Walter B. Knight. *Knight's Master Book of 4,000 Illustrations*, p.315.

> to make the choice of a gift. He said he was content and wanted nothing. But on being urged to make some request, he asked for the power to do a great deal of good in the world without [ever] knowing it.
>
> And so, ever afterward his shadow, when it fell behind him where he could not see it, had wondrous healing power; but when it was cast before him where he could see it, it had no such power.[39]

What an example of humility! When given the opportunity to choose some great power, this man chose one that would only benefit others with no credit to himself!

12–154

HUMILITY

Jude 1-2

The Secret of Success

(POSB, Note 1, point 2)

Humility is nothing to boast about. It would actually be a contradiction! But some Christians do take pride in being humble. And they scare away a whole lot more fish than they catch.

> A little boy was out fishing with only a switch for a pole and a bent pin for a hook, but he was catching many fish. A city fellow who had spent much time fishing without any success...came across the boy with his long string of fish, and he asked the boy the reason of his success. The boy said, "The secret of it all is that I keep myself out of sight." We [too] must keep ourselves out of sight if we desire [success,] to be a blessing to others.[40]

The true believer or minister is a person who humbles himself before God and others, who surrenders to Jesus Christ and serves Him wholeheartedly.

12–155

JESUS CHRIST

2 Peter 3:8-10

Are You Ready for His Return?

(POSB, Note 1, point 2)

Waiting on the Lord is something that requires great patience. But it is an eternal mistake to live as if He will *not* return, as the following poem illustrates:

> 'TWAS THE NIGHT BEFORE JESUS CAME
>
> 'Twas the night before Jesus came and all through the house,
> Not a creature was praying, not one in the house.

39 *J. H. Bomberger.* Paul Lee Tan. *Encyclopedia of 7,700 Illustrations: Signs of the Times*, p.572.
40 *Junior Challenge.* Walter B. Knight. *Knight's Master Book of 4,000 Illustrations*, p.313.

Their Bibles were lain on the shelf without care,
    In hopes that Jesus would not come there.

The children were dressing to crawl into bed,
    Not once ever kneeling or bowing a head.
And Mom in her rocker with baby on her lap,
    Was watching the Late Show while I took a nap.

When out of the East there arose such a clatter,
    I sprang to my feet to see what was the matter.
Away to the window I flew like a flash,
    Tore open the shutters and threw up the sash!

When what to my wondering eyes should appear,
    But angels proclaiming that Jesus was here.
With a light like the sun sending forth a bright ray,
    I knew in a moment this must be THE DAY!

The light of His face made me cover my head.
    It was Jesus! Returning, just like He had said.
And though I possessed worldly wisdom and wealth,
    I cried when I saw Him in spite of myself.

In the Book of Life which He held in His hand,
    Was written the name of every saved man.
He spoke not a word as He searched for my name;
    When He said, "It's not here" my head hung in shame.

The people whose names had been written with love,
    He gathered to take to His Father above.
With those who were ready, He rose without a sound,
    While all the rest were left standing around.

I fell to my knees, but it was too late;
    I had waited too long and thus sealed my fate.
I stood and I cried as they rose out of sight;
    Oh, if only I had been ready tonight.
In the words of this poem the meaning is clear;
    The coming of Jesus is drawing near.
There's only one life and when comes the last call,
    We'll find that the Bible was true after all![41]

41 Ken Krivohalavek. *Rejoicin' an' Repentin'*. (Olathe, KS: KLK Ministries, 2002), p.122.

PRACTICAL ILLUSTRATIONS

12–156

JESUS CHRIST

1 John 5:9-15

Believing What You Hear

(POSB, Note 1, point 4)

What is the secret to finding life in Christ? A person simply has to believe the witness that God gave us about His Son and then accept Christ as Lord and Savior. One preacher explains it like this:

> [Salvation] is the gift of God. So is the air, but you have to breathe it. So is bread, but you have to eat it. So is water, but you have to drink it. So how do we accept this gift? Not by a feeling, for "faith comes by hearing, and hearing by the Word of God" (Rom.10:17). It is not for me to sit down and wait for faith to come upon me with a strong feeling of some kind. Rather, [salvation] comes when we take God at his word.[42]

12–157

JESUS CHRIST

1 Peter 3:18-22

Blameless in Christ

(POSB, Note 1, point 3)

Jesus Christ died for our sins, accepting the guilt and punishment of sin for all men. The author Max Lucado adds tremendous insight to this wonderful truth.

> The decision had been made. The troops had been deployed and the battleships were on their way. Nearly three million soldiers were preparing to slam against Hitler's Atlantic wall in France. D-Day was set in motion. Responsibility for the invasion fell squarely on the four-starred shoulders of General Dwight D. Eisenhower....A correspondent wrote that as Eisenhower watched the C-47s take off and disappear into the darkness, his hands were sunk deeply into his pockets and his eyes were full of tears.
>
> The general then went to his quarters and sat at his desk. He took a pen and paper and wrote a message—a message which would be delivered to the White House in the event of a defeat.
>
> It was as brief as it was courageous. "Our landings...have failed...the troops, the Air, and the Navy did all that bravery and devotion to duty could do. If any blame or fault attaches itself to the attempt it was mine alone." ("D-Day Recalling Military Gamble that Shaped History," Time, 28 May 1984, 16).
>
> It could be argued that the greatest act of courage that day was not in a cockpit or foxhole, but at a desk when the one at the top took responsibility for the ones below. When the one in charge took the blame—even before the blame needed to be taken.
>
> Rare leader, this general. Unusual, this display of courage. He modeled a quality seldom seen in our society of lawsuits, dismissals, and divorces. Most of us are willing to take credit for the good we do. Some are willing to take the rap for the bad we do. But few will assume responsibilities for the mistakes of others. Still fewer will shoulder the blame for mistakes yet uncommitted.
>
> Eisenhower did. As a result, he became a hero.
>
> Jesus did. As a result, He's our Savior.[43]

---

42 Michael P. Green. *Illustrations for Biblical Preaching,* #445.

43 Max Lucado. *And the Angels Were Silent.* (Portland, OR: Multnomah Press, 1992), pp.27-28.

12–158

JESUS CHRIST

1 Peter 2:4-8

(POSB, Note 4, point 2)

Build on the Sure Foundation

Have you ever built a house or worked with someone who did? If so, you can easily recall the hours of planning, the many decisions to be made, the long days of construction, and the seemingly endless extra jobs that were needed to keep things on track. Detailed thought is required to build a house. It is *not* all fun and games, and it is *not* easy. It has even been said that the true test of a marriage is building a house together and surviving it! But it *can* be done if you have the right foundation. The right foundation is key to a strong building.

Just like building a house, the key to building a successful Christian life and surviving all the trials is having a firm foundation—that is, having your life built on Jesus Christ. Those who reject Jesus Christ as the chief cornerstone are doomed to failure, doomed to destruction and condemnation for their disobedience.

12–159

JESUS CHRIST

1 Peter 2:4-8

(POSB, Note 1)

The Danger of Rejecting Christ

Why would anyone want to reject Jesus Christ? For some, it is because Christ does not fit into their concept of a world leader or savior, a point well illustrated in the life of a former American leader.

> In the fall of 1775, the manager of Baltimore's largest hotel refused lodging to a man dressed as a farmer, because he thought this fellow's lowly appearance would discredit his inn. So the man left and took a room elsewhere. Later, the innkeeper discovered that he had turned away none other than the Vice President of the United States, Thomas Jefferson!
>
> Immediately he sent a note to the famed patriot, asking him to return and be his guest. Jefferson replied by instructing his messenger as follows: "Tell him I have already engaged a room. I value his good intentions highly, but if he has no place for a dirty American farmer, he has none for the Vice President of the United States."[44]

44 *Our Daily Bread.* Paul Lee Tan. *Encyclopedia of 7,700 Illustrations: Signs of the Times*, p.649.

PRACTICAL ILLUSTRATIONS

12–160

JESUS CHRIST

1 Peter 2:21-25

(POSB, Note 3, point 2)

No One Ever Cared Like Jesus

What a great blessing it is to have a Shepherd like our Lord Jesus. Knowing and experiencing His love that has no limits and His power that keeps and protects us *should* humble us—to think that He would want to care for us.

> I frequently go out at night to walk alone under the stars and remind myself of His majesty and might. Looking up at the star-studded sky I remember that at least 250,000,000 x 250,000,000 such bodies—each larger than our sun, one of the smallest of the stars—have been scattered across the vast spaces of the universe by His hand. I recall that the planet earth, which is my temporary home for a few short years, is so minute a speck of matter in space that if it were possible to transport our most powerful telescope to our nearest neighbor star, Alpha Centauri, and look back this way, the earth could not be seen, even with the aid of that powerful instrument.
>
> All of this is a bit humbling. It drains the "ego" from a man and puts things in proper perspective. It makes me see myself as a mere mite of material in an enormous universe. Yet the staggering fact remains that Christ the Creator of such an enormous universe of overwhelming magnitude, deigns to call Himself my Shepherd and invites me to consider myself His sheep—His special object of affection and attention. Who better could care for me?[45]

As the hymn-writer Charles Weigle reminds us, "No one ever cared for me—like Jesus."[46] Why trust your care to anyone else?

12–161

JESUS CHRIST

1 John 1:10–2:2

(POSB, Note 3, point 2)

Our Judge and Our Savior

Imagine that you have just committed a capital offense. You cannot afford a lawyer, so you are appointed an attorney by the court. The prosecutor is mean-spirited and has an agenda to convict you. He will settle for nothing less than the death penalty. Now, take your place in court.

> The bailiff shouts, "All rise for the King of Kings and Lord of Lords, the Righteous Judge of Israel!" You stand to your feet and are humbled and fearful. This Judge now has power over your life. You know that you are guilty and have already reconciled yourself to the worst-case scenario—being found guilty and put to death.
>
> As you take your seat, you wonder where your court-appointed attorney might be. He has yet to take his seat next to yours. On the other side of the courtroom is your adversary. He is the one who wants to see you put to death. He walks briskly up to the

---

45 W. Phillip Keller. *A Shepherd Looks at Psalm 23*. (Grand Rapids, MI: Zondervan Publishing House, 1979), p.18.

46 Assigned to *Singspiration*. Division of Zondervan Corporation, Nashville, TN, 1932 (renewal 1960).

Judge and says, "Your honor, this man is guilty of a capital offense. He is a sinner. He is a hypocrite. I know that he is now a Christian, but he used to be in my employment as an agent of evil. I want justice and I want it now. I demand that you find him guilty and put him to death!"

Your heart sinks. Your court-appointed attorney has still not taken his seat next to you. All of a sudden the Judge leaves his chair and walks over to you. You expect him to condemn you without a trial, but instead he says, "I am going to take your case. I know you are guilty, but if you recall, I have already paid your penalty with the nail prints in my hands. I declare to you, to your prosecutor, and to this court that I find you—NOT GUILTY! Case dismissed."

What a profound truth this is! Though Satan stands before God accusing you, the genuine believer can take heart, for his Judge is also his Savior!

12–162

JUDGMENT

2 Peter 3:1-7

(POSB, Note 5, point 3)

The Danger of Ignorance

Scoffers are *willingly ignorant.* Like the proverbial ostrich, they choose to hide their heads in the sands of denial.

Legend has it that the ostrich overheard Chicken Little say the sky was falling. Fearing for his life, the ostrich hid his head in the sand. Thinking to himself, the ostrich said, "I'll be safe if I do not see anything bad."

And so, the ostrich kept his head in the sand. One of his animal friends walked by and said, "Ostrich, why is your head in the sand?" With a voice muffled by the sand, the ostrich said, "Chicken Little said the sky is falling. If I can't see it I'll be safe."

"But Ostrich" said the animal friend, "I think Chicken Little is wrong. The sky is not falling. Why don't you look up for yourself and see?" And the friend walked on.

Another animal came upon the ostrich who still had his head hidden in the sand. "Ostrich, why is your head buried in the sand?" said the animal. Again, with a muffled voice, "Because if I can't see the end of the world, I won't get hurt." "Great idea" said the lion. Then he took a vicious bite and had the ostrich for his dinner.

The scoffer is a lot like the ostrich in this story. He may deny that he is in eternal danger, but that does not change the truth. One day the world *will* end, and Christ will judge every person. Keep your head up! Look heavenward and accept Christ's salvation. It, too, is very real.

12–163

JUDGMENT

2 Peter 2:10-22

(POSB, Note 15, point 3)

God Cannot Be Mocked

The false teacher will not escape God's judgment. He may mock for a time, but God is not unaware. Here is a dramatic story of God's wrath upon one mocker.

Seth Joshua, one of the leaders of the great Welsh revival of generations ago once arrived in a town where he was scheduled to preach and found placards everywhere announcing "the Great Seth Joshua." They told all about him but were in reality advertising a stage imitation of the minister at a local theatre that night. Grotesque drawings promised much fun at the expense of this servant of the Lord. That night the theatre was packed and the crowd cheered as the actor came on the stage in perfect imitation of preaching Joshua.

The actor raised his arms as he circled the stage burlesquing the Bible and the evangelist.

The third time around the actor fell with a thud and a hushed audience soon discovered that he was dead.

God will not hold his wrath forever.[47]

No one can mock God. No one.

12–164

LEGACY

2 Peter 1:5-15

(POSB, Note 3, point 3)

Touching Others for Christ

When you leave this earth, what will people remember about you? What kind of legacy will you leave behind? Perhaps a great one, like this man who lost his battle with cancer but won the war for the souls of men.

Bob was a believer who made it his life's task to memorize God's Word and live by it. He was known by many as the walking Bible. Being full of God's Word, Bob never lacked a good word for anybody who needed encouragement or hope. Bob took to heart this Psalm:

> **"Thy word have I hid in mine heart, that I might not sin against thee" (Ps.119:11).**

Eventually, cancer overtook Bob and he went on to heaven. But not before he convinced many others to join him there in due time. Bob didn't own a big business, start a movement, or build a skyscraper. He didn't even have his name inscribed on a brass plate anywhere. But it *was* inscribed in the Book of Life. And everyone Bob talked to knew it.

---

47 Walter B. Knight. *Knight's Master Book of 4,000 Illustrations*, p.350.

What did Bob leave behind? Touched lives, disciples who caught the vision to memorize and live out the Word of God. A person's greatest legacy is seen in the people he leaves behind. What will your legacy be?

12–165

LIGHT

1 John 1:6-7

(POSB, Note 1, point 4)

Exposing the Darkness

The believer is strongly warned. He cannot live in the darkness of this world and expect the light of God to guide him throughout life. Here is the story of one man who tried.

Aaron was a salesman with a strong personality and lots of charisma. Image was very important to him. He loved the applause of men and would feed his ego by seeking out popular places to make an appearance. Trying to become "one of the guys" was his excuse for compromising his values to sell more products.

On Sunday mornings, he went to church. In public, he even talked like a Christian. But in reality, Aaron led a double life and did whatever he felt necessary to get ahead in business. When it came to his Christian life, Aaron "talked the talk" but didn't "walk the walk." It did not take long for his double standards and hypocrisy to affect the reputation of the business.

Aaron's employer soon took him aside and said "Aaron, I really appreciate all the good things you do, like meeting your sales goals. But for your own good, I'm going to ask you to take a break from working outside the office. I want you to take a close look at your lifestyle. You are making choices that no longer affect just you alone. Until you can make some changes in your lifestyle, I'm taking you off the road."

Aaron hung his head in shame. His employer had seen past his smooth exterior into his dark inner self. The light of God's Spirit had exposed Aaron's true heart.

When God shines His light on you, what will He expose in your life?

12–166

LIGHT

1 John 1:1-5

(POSB, Note 5)

Jesus Is the Light of the World

The world has become accustomed to the darkness of sin and shame, but God's light is totally pure. There is no darkness in Him. Therefore, His light reveals our imperfections.

When the new technology of high-definition television came on the scene, it had an immediate effect on how things were done in the studio. Low-tech television had such poor picture resolution that the visual details of a studio did not show up on the screen. Actors and newscasters wore thick pancake makeup to hide wrinkles, moles, and blemishes, but the makeup was invisible to the relatively crude camera. Fake books rested on shelves, and cardboard backdrops with painted wood grain stood as walls. Still, with low-tech television, the viewer was none the wiser. Says Jim Fenhagen, a set designer who works for the major networks, "With old TV, you can get away with murder."

But high-definition television, using high-resolution digital technology, changed all that. The studio camera picks up everything from scratches on the desk to blemishes on the skin. That has forced a change in how things are done.

When we come to God, we come to the one who sees us as we really are. We must be completely truthful with Him.[48]

Has God's light filled the dark rooms of your heart?

12–167

LOVE

1 John 3:1-3

(POSB, Note 2, point 3)

The Comfort of God's Love

The believer can find great comfort and hope in God's love. One day, every believer will be permanently changed into the image of Christ. The world may shake around us, but God's plan for us is unshakable.

In 1995, a devastating earthquake shook the city of Kobe, Japan. Thousands of people lost their lives and billions of dollars of damage was done to buildings and roads. It was reported that a Christian church in Kobe was also destroyed, but in its courtyard, a statue of Christ remained perfectly erect. Word of the statue's survival spread all across Japan. As people came to examine it, the statue became a symbol of hope to a people whose world had fallen apart.

There is a very practical point in this story: no matter how shaky it gets here on earth, one day every believer shall be like Christ—incorruptible, never decaying, deteriorating, or dying. We will be transformed from brokenness to stability, from death to life, from sorrow to joy.—SOURCE UNKNOWN

When your world gets shaky, remember the glory that awaits you in your permanent home in heaven.

12–168

LOVE

1 John 4:7-21

(POSB, Note 7, point 3)

Focusing on People

Jesus Christ did not come into the world to save an institution—He came to save people. Walter B. Knight stresses this point with this thought-provoking story.

A budding high-school orator delivered Lincoln's Gettysburg Address. Calmly he began, "Fourscore and seven years ago." He glowed with fervency when he came to the climactic words "...that government *of* the people, *by* the people, and *for* the people

48 Craig B. Larson, Editor. *Choice Contemporary Stories & Illustrations for Preachers, Teachers & Writers,* #247, p. 281.

shall not perish from the earth!" The audience applauded...An old man hobbled slowly through the crowd and said to the young orator, "You did a grand job, son! You will be interested to know that I was present at Gettysburg when Lincoln delivered that memorable speech.... But, son, you didn't say it just like Lincoln did.

"You said, 'Government *of* the people, *by* the people, and *for* the people.' When Lincoln spoke these words...he said, 'Government of the *people*, by the *people*, and for the *people*.' Your emphasis is on [the] prepositions [not on the people]!" [49]

As believers, we too must remember not to focus upon things, places, or organizations but upon people. God commands it!

12–169

LOVE

1 John 3:10-17

(POSB, Note 5)

Getting Rid of Anger

Hatred or bitterness in the life of a believer is like a cancer that grows at an incredible rate of speed. Is there a cure for the deadly effects of hate? Yes. It is called love. How does love diffuse hate? Abraham Lincoln had a unique way of dealing with such issues.

Few people have the tact that President Lincoln had, when dealing with a situation that tempts one to use harsh measures.

When the darkest clouds of the Civil War were hovering over the capital, many things done by the generals were not approved by either Lincoln or Secretary Stanton. Lincoln would take a long time to ponder over situations, but Stanton would, at times, lose his temper and explode. One day Stanton came to see Lincoln about the doings of a certain general. Listening quietly, Lincoln let Stanton show his anger, and when the latter exclaimed, "I would like to write him a letter and tell him what I think of him!" Lincoln remarked quietly, "Well, why not do so? Sit down and write him a letter, saying all you have said to me."

Stanton was surprised for he thought that President Lincoln would object to this. He declared that he would take the President at his word.

Two days later he brought Lincoln the letter he had written, and read it to him. When Stanton had finished, Lincoln smiled and remarked, "That is all right. You have said all you told me you would. Now, what are you going to do with this letter?"

"Why, I am going to give it to him, of course."

"I wouldn't," replied the President quietly. "Throw it in the waste basket."

"What, after spending two days on it," exclaimed Stanton.

"Yes. It took you two days to write it, and it did you a lot of good. You feel a great deal better now, and that is all that is necessary."

The letter went into the waste basket, and Stanton learned an important lesson.[50]

Perhaps there is someone in your path who needs your love, not your wrath, today.

49 Walter B. Knight. *Knight's Treasury of 2,000 Illustrations.* (Grand Rapids, MI: Eerdmans Publishing Company, 1992), p.216.

50 *Young People.* Walter B. Knight. *Knight's Master Book of 4,000 Illustrations*, pp.177-178.

Practical Illustrations

12–170

Love

2 John 5-6

(POSB, Note 1)

Love Your Enemies

Love your enemies. Can that command possibly be in the Bible? The capacity to love those who are impossible to love is one of the great distinguishing marks of Christianity. Here is the story of a man who put this principle into action.

> Louis Zamperini...a former Olympic runner, who ditched his plane off Oahu Hawaii, during World War II and drifted 2,000 miles in 47 days on a life raft, was picked up by a Japanese vessel. He was a prisoner for the two remaining years of the war. He was starved and tortured by his captors...At home he was given up for dead. He is in the possession of his own death certificate signed by President Roosevelt.
>
> Zamperini said he left Japan in 1945 with hatred in his heart against his captors. But in 1949 he was saved at one of Billy Graham's meetings in Los Angeles. "There is such a change in my life that I feel I have a duty to perform." Zamperini told his friends. "That duty is to return to Japan and tell them of the saving power of the Lord Jesus Christ."[51]

Love covers a multitude of sins—even those of your enemies.

12–171

Love

2 John 5-6

(POSB, Note 2, point 15)

Putting Love into Action

Love is an action word, a behavior, a way of life.

> Bruce Thielemann...told of a conversation with an active layman, who mentioned, "You preachers talk a lot about giving, but when you get right down to it, it all comes down to basin theology."
>
> Thielemann asked, "Basin theology? What's that?"
>
> The layman replied, "Remember what Pilate did when he had the chance to acquit Jesus? He called for a basin and washed his hands of the whole thing. But Jesus, the night before His death, called for a basin and proceeded to wash the feet of the disciples. It all comes down to basin theology: Which one will you use?"[52]

When it comes to loving others, you can wash your hands of the whole affair as Pilate did, or you can humble yourself and love others as Jesus did. Which way of life are *you* living?

---

51 Walter B. Knight. *Knight's Master Book of 4,000 Illustrations*, pp.176-177.

52 Craig B. Larson, Editor. *Illustrations for Preaching & Teaching*, p.220.

12–172

LOVE

2 Peter 1:5-15

(POSB, Note 1, point 7)

The Power of Sacrificial Love

Who can fully explain the power of sacrificial love—love that gives beyond measure? The strength of God's love simply cannot be overcome by evil.

> After the U.S.S. Pueblo was captured by the North Koreans, the eighty-two surviving crew members were thrown into a brutal captivity. In one particular instance thirteen of the men were required to sit in a rigid manner around a table for hours. After several hours the door was violently flung open and a North Korean guard brutally beat the man in the first chair with the butt of his rifle. The next day, as each man sat at his assigned place, again the door was thrown open and the man in the first chair was brutally beaten. On the third day it happened again to the same man. Knowing the man could not survive, another young sailor took his place. When the door was flung open the guard automatically beat the new victim senseless. For weeks, each day a new man stepped forward to sit in that horrible chair, knowing full well what would happen. At last the guards gave up in exasperation. They were unable to beat that kind of sacrificial love.[53]

How far would you be willing to go in the name of love?

12–173

LOVE

1 John 3:10-17

(POSB, Note 7)

Willing to Take the Risk

A good way to gauge how much you love God is to consider how much you are willing to give for the cause of Christ. A man named Andy proved his love in a very real way.

> Years ago, Andy, a graduate school student from the mid-west, was moved by the need of another brother. The new semester had come and one of his friends was $150.00 short of what he needed to stay in school. Andy didn't have to think twice about what to do. He gave his friend the money.
>
> Andy made a tremendous sacrifice. Like most students, he did not have a large reserve of cash to share. In fact, a year later, Andy had to drop out of school for a year to earn more money to finish his own education. Did he ever regret giving that money to his friend? Not in any way. He later said, "To have done anything else would have been sin. My brother had a need and I had the privilege of helping meet that need. Don't worry about me. God will take care of me too." And God did. Andy finished his degree a year later—just in time...in God's time...in God's way...with God's provision.

The believer never loses when his motive for action is love. Love is always worth the risk.

---

53 Michael P. Green. *Illustrations for Biblical Preaching*, pp.226-227.

12–174

LUST

2 Peter 3:1-7

(POSB, Note 3)

Living on the Brink of Disaster

People who scoff at the truth of the gospel are living on the brink of disaster, as seen clearly in the following story.

> As part of a circus act, a man would place his head in a tiger's mouth! He advanced to the tiger and the tiger opened his mouth. While the crowd watched in breathless wonder and horror, the man thrust his head in the open mouth, paused a moment, then slowly withdrew his head from the place of danger and backed from the cage. As he shut the door, the tiger leaped against the bars with terrific force.
>
> Such a foolhardy stunt was sure to attract much attention, and many prophesied that some day that man would pay for his foolishness. Their utterance was [ful]filled. In a small town in northern Pennsylvania the man met his doom. While his head was in the tiger's mouth, those powerful jaws closed on him, and before several bullets ended the tiger's life, the man was a corpse.
>
> This takes us in thought to two verses in the Epistle of James: "But every man is tempted, when he is drawn away of his own lust, and enticed. Then when lust hath conceived, it bringeth forth sin; and sin, when it is finished, bringeth forth death."[54]

Lust can turn anyone's head and blind him to danger. Is your head on straight or is it in the mouth of the tiger?

12–175

LUST

1 Peter 2:11-12

(POSB, Note 2, point 3)

The Overpowering Grip of Lust

Believers must abstain from fleshly lusts, for they "war against the soul." And lusts that enslave are lusts that will eventually destroy a person's life. There is no such thing as compromising with lust. You cannot partially abstain. Walter B. Knight remarks:

> A missionary...was asked, "Have you gotten those terrible cannibals to a place yet where they do not eat each other?" "No, [came the reply] but we have succeeded in getting them to use knives and forks!"[55]

54 L.L. Wightman, in *Gospel Herald.* Walter B. Knight. *Knight's Master Book of 4,000 Illustrations*, p.626.
55 Walter B. Knight. *Knight's Master Book of 4,000 Illustrations*, p.713.

12–176

Marriage

1 Peter 3:1-6

(POSB, Note 1)

Actions Preach Louder Than Words

God's will is for a husband and wife to stay together. But what if the husband is not a believer? God's way is still best. Listen to this story about a wife who won her husband to Christ.

> A Hindu woman was converted, chiefly by hearing the Word of God read. She suffered very much persecution from her husband. One day a missionary asked her, "When your husband is angry and persecutes you, what do you do?"
>
> She replied: "Well, sir, I cook his food better; when he complains, I sweep the floor cleaner; and when he speaks unkindly, I answer him mildly. I try, sir, to show him that when I became a Christian, I became a better wife and a better mother."
>
> The consequence of this was that, while the husband could withstand all the preaching of the missionary, he could not stand the practical preaching of his wife, and gave his heart to God with her.[56]

A lost person seldom cares how much you know; he really wants to know how much you care.

12–177

Mercy

1 Peter 2:9-10

(POSB, Note 3, point 2)

Who Will Pay for Your Sin?

Where would we be without the mercy of God? Under severe judgment, condemned to an eternity in hell, apart from God. But once we confess our sins and acknowledge our need for the Savior, God's mercy floods our souls. A clear example of mercy in action is seen below.

> [T]here lived an earnest Christian man who became a magistrate. One morning there appeared before him in the court a friend of his youth, who had strayed from the paths of righteousness and had committed an offense against the law of the land.
>
> Those who knew the relationship between the two men expected the magistrate to deal with the man mercifully, and they were very much surprised when they heard that the sentence was a heavy fine. But they were more surprised when the magistrate went to the officer of the court, and took from his own pocket the money to pay the fine. He did his duty as a magistrate, and upheld the law, but he also showed something of the mercy of God...when he paid the penalty for his friend.
>
> There is little wonder that the law-breaker was broken-hearted in his repentance. Jesus gave Himself for you. Have you given yourself to Him?[57]

56 *Evangelical Visitor.* Walter B. Knight. *Knight's Master Book of 4,000 Illustrations,* p.68.
57 *Peniel Herald.* Walter B. Knight. *3,000 Illustrations for Christian Service,* p.437.

12–178

OBEDIENCE

2 Peter 3:15-18

(POSB, Note 2)

Beware—Lest You Stray

The Christian believer is without excuse when it comes to knowing the truth. God has given His Word, the Holy Bible, to the believer; and He has given the Holy Spirit to guide the believer into the truth. Once you know the truth it is your duty to act upon it. Here is a stirring story that will encourage you to practice what you know.

> You probably have heard played many times "The Stars and Stripes Forever," a spirited march by John Phillip Sousa. Sitting in his hotel room one summer evening, Mr. Sousa heard a hand organ man in the street below playing this, his favorite march, in a slow, dragging manner. He dashed to the street. "Here, here," he called to the sleepy, lazy grinder, "that is no way to play that march!"
>
> He seized the handle of the organ and turned it vigorously. The music rushed out, spirited and snappy. The hand organ man bowed low and smiled. The next night Mr. Sousa heard the organ again. This time the tempo was right. Looking out the window, he saw a great crowd gathering about the player. Over the organ on a large card was the grinder's name, and under it, "Pupil of John Philip Sousa."
>
> The organ grinder was quick to put into practice what he had learned, and he was proud to have learned from such a great teacher....And you—are you ashamed to let it be known that you are a pupil of the Lord Jesus; and do you put into practice the things you learn of Him?[58]

You have learned the truth. Now, beware—lest you stray!

12–179

OBEDIENCE

1 Peter 1:13-16

(POSB, Note 2)

Getting Rid of Selfish Desires

Is anything preventing you from being obedient to God's call upon your life? Excuses come and go, but there is no excuse for not obeying God. The reason obedience is such a challenge is because of "I." "I" want this and "I" want that. See if you can relate to this man's tragic story of how "I" got in the way of obeying God.

> "I have enjoyed the meetings this week, but I am sorry I attended them," said a well-to-do businessman to a minister. "Why?" asked the astonished minister. "Here's why. These meetings have reminded me afresh that I have missed God's best for my life. I was called to Africa. I intended to answer God's call."
>
> "I began to earn money for my passage and outfit. I earned more and more money. I stayed and entered business. Today I am the owner of a large business concern. I have everything money can buy. I have a beautiful home and a lovely wife and

---

58 Walter B. Knight. *Knight's Master Book of 4,000 Illustrations*, pp.440-441.

children. Down in my heart, however, there is a great void. My life has been a failure, not from the standpoint of the world, but from God's point of view!"[59]

Are you obeying God from *His* point of view?

12–180

OBEDIENCE

1 John 2:3-6

(POSB, Note 3)

Keeping God's Word

The believer not only must *know* what God says to do, but he also must *do* what God says, as cleverly illustrated in this story.

Dr. W. D. Robertson was once approached by a lady who objected to any kind of ritual in church service. She said, "I hear that you are introducing some dreadful innovations in your church service." "Indeed," he replied, "what innovations have we introduced?"

"Oh," she said, "I hear that you read the Commandments in your service." "Is that all you heard!" Dr. Robertson replied. "We have introduced a far greater innovation than that. We try to keep the Commandments."[60]

Are you a keeper of God's commandments or just a "knower"?

12–181

OBEDIENCE

1 John 2:7-11

(POSB, Note 3, point 2)

The Need to Be Accountable

A very practical way to love your brother is to agree to hold him accountable. How is this an act of love and obedience?

Joe and Don were true believers and good friends who loved the Lord and wanted to be sure they did not waver from the path of righteousness. Seeing many of their friends fall into sin, they felt convicted to protect themselves. They, too, were human and struggled with temptations.

After praying about how to stay accountable, they agreed to meet weekly for a four question "check-up." The first question dealt with their relationship with God: "Is it growing?" The second question addressed their relationships with family and friends: "Are they growing?" The third question pressed into an area where most men have difficulties: "Have you had any problems with your thought-life?" The fourth question kept everything in perspective: "Have you been absolutely truthful in answering the first three questions?"

---

59 *Prairie Overcomer.* Walter B. Knight. *Knight's Treasury of 2,000 Illustrations,* p.241.

60 *Earnest Worker.* Walter B. *Knight. Knight's Master Book of 4,000 Illustrations,* p.438.

What did this honesty do for Joe and Don? While other men's marriages were drowning, their marriages were making healthy strides. When other men were slipping in their Christian testimony at work, their testimony was real. And where other men lived in the perverted fantasies of their minds, Joe and Don were working at captivating every thought and subjecting it to the obedience of Christ (2 Cor.10:5).

The most loving thing you can do for a brother or sister in Christ is to hold him or her accountable. The most loving thing you can do for yourself is to have others hold you accountable. Remember, true love is not prideful; it does not rejoice in someone's wrongdoing. Instead, love is kind and patient, helpful and caring.

12–182

OBEDIENCE

1 John 5:1-5

(POSB, Note 2, point 2)

Nothing Else Will Do

A very practical proof of the new birth is the desire to obey God.

One day the father of young twins walked into their playroom and was struck by the whirlwind that took place while he was out. "What a mess. Guys, before you come down for supper, I want you to pick up all these toys and put them back where they belong." said the father as he left the room.

One of the twins got a gleam in his eye. "I'm going to surprise dad. I'm going to build him something special with these blocks: maybe a bridge...or a giant tower."

The other twin looked at his brother and blinked a couple of times. Then he looked at the blocks and said, "Not me. I'm going to do what Daddy said. I want to eat!"

How many times do you substitute obedience with your own idea, thinking it will turn out better? God doesn't need a favor; He doesn't need anything? But we desperately need to obey Him to receive the blessings He has in mind for us.

12–183

OBEDIENCE

1 John 2:15-17

(POSB, Note 3)

The Path to Safety

The *bottom line* for the believer is this: If you do God's will, you will live forever. A lot of people are not going to make it to heaven because they want to do things their own way instead of God's way. In short, they are not obedient, not willing to listen to God. But listen closely to this story.

An aviation cadet, on a practice flight, temporarily stricken blind, in panic radioed that message to his control officer. This officer radioed back, "Follow my instructions implicitly." After keeping the blinded cadet circling the field until the whole field was cleared and an ambulance had arrived, the control officer radioed: "Now lose altitude." "Now bank sharply." "You're coming onto the field now."

The cadet brought his plane to a perfect landing, was saved, and later his sight returned [--all because he had followed instructions. This is] all the Lord is asking of us...implicit obedience. [61]

Sometimes you may feel like this pilot—scared and unsure of where life is taking you. But as a believer, you have God's promise: If you are obedient, God will bring you home safely to live with Him forever.

12–184

OBEDIENCE

1 Peter 4:1-6

(POSB, Note 2)

The Value of Following God's Will

Doing the will of God keeps us from going our own way. Have you reached a place in your Christian walk where you can do God's business while trusting that He will take care of yours? This story echoes that thought.

Queen Elizabeth asked a rich English merchant to go on a mission for the crown. The merchant [protested]....saying that such a long absence would be fatal to his business. "You take care of my business," replied the Queen, "and I will take care of yours."

When he returned, he found that through the patronage and care of the Queen, his business had increased in volume and he was richer than when he left. So every business can afford to place Christ's interests first, for the promise is clear and unmistakable. Do Christ's will, and He will look after your welfare.[62]

12–185

PEACE

2 Peter 1:1-4

(POSB, Note 3, point 3)

Jesus Christ: The Source of Peace

When Christ fills a heart, His peace will overflow. This story emphasizes this great truth.

A much-beloved man, a leader in a little community of Christian students, lived such a life of serenity and peace that all his student-companions wondered. At length they determined to approach him and ask to be told the secret of his calm. They said: "We are harassed by many temptations, which appeal to us so often and so strongly that they give us no rest. You seem to live untroubled by these things, and we want to know your secret. Don't the temptations that harass our souls come knocking at the door of your heart?"

---

61 Tom M. Olson, in *Sunday School Times*. Walter B. Knight. *Knight's Master Book of 4,000 Illustrations*, pp.443-444.

62 A.C.D., in *Choice Gleanings Calendar.* Walter B. Knight. *Knight's Master Book of 4,000 Illustrations*, p.731.

> He replied: "My children, I do know something of the things of which you speak. The temptations that trouble you do come, making their appeal to me. But when they knock at the door of my heart, I answer, "The place is occupied."[63]

If your heart is occupied by the Lord Jesus Christ, sin will not find a resting place there.

12–186

PEACE

1 Peter 3:10-12

Striving Against the Odds

(POSB, Note 3)

Peace may not always be possible, but we must strive for it in every way we can. Zig Ziglar illustrates:

> A little guy was confronted by three bullies, any one of whom could have obliterated him, and they were giving him some evidence that they had that plan in mind. The little guy was very bright, so he backed away from the three bullies, drew a line in the dirt, backed up a few more steps, looked into the eyes of the biggest of the three and said, "Now, you just step across that line." Confidently, the big bully did exactly that, and the little guy just grinned and said, "Now, we're both on the same side."[64]

Did the boy make the bullies laugh and bring peace? We don't know. But the point is that he didn't give up *trying* to make peace. Neither should the believer, even when the odds are against him.

12–187

PEACE

1 Peter 5:10-14

Unshakable Peace

(POSB, Note 5, point 2)

One of the great provisions of the gospel is the very real possibility of peace in some of the most troubling circumstances. Listen to this graphic story.

> Two artists put upon canvas their concepts of peace. One artist painted a placid rural scene in the center of which was a country home. Adjacent to the home were fertile fields and an abundant harvest. The undulating roads stretched in different directions from the home toward the horizon. A lazy haze hovered over glen and dale. One could almost hear the rustle of the ripened wheat, swayed with the kiss of the gentle breeze. A friendly sun shone upon the blissful picture of calm and contentment. Cows lay lazily under a shade tree, chewing their cud.
>
> The other artist gave a totally different concept of peace. A destroying tempest raged in his painting. Trees swayed to and fro on the storm-lashed mountain-side and in the valley. The sky was ominous and gloomy, relieved only by the zigzag flashes of

63 *Methodist Recorder.* Walter B. Knight. *Knight's Master Book of 4,000 Illustrations*, p.464.

64 Alice Gray. *More Stories for the Heart.* (Sisters, OR: Multnomah Press, 1997), p. 109.

lightning. A roaring waterfall lunged furiously over the precipice, working disaster in the valley below!

Why could the artist call this violent, turbulent scene a representation of peace? On a rock projecting from the cliff, sheltered by an overhanging boulder, sat a little bird calmly on its nest, seemingly unmindful of the howling storm or of the raging waters which plunged downward nearby. There the little bird sat in peace, with no fear, unperturbed and undisturbed![65]

Does your peace come and go according to your circumstances? Or do you possess the peace of God that transcends *all* circumstances? The choice is yours!

12–188

PERSECUTION

1 Peter 2:18-20

(POSB, Note 4, point 2)

Breaking the Bonds of Sin

During the days of American slavery, teaching a slave to read or write was considered a crime. The slave-code made learning difficult for the slave—if not impossible. Why was this so? Seeking to keep the upper hand, the cruel slave owners refused to allow the light of knowledge to enter the minds of their slaves. Most probably, the slave owners feared that if slaves could read and write, it would only be a matter of time before their slaves would rise up and revolt. To prevent this possible outbreak, the slave owners ruled with an intimidating hand. It was a hand that attempted to squash any attempt for the slaves to gain an education. The slave owners wanted to maintain their power by keeping their slaves ignorant—uninformed of the vast amount of knowledge that was awaiting them. In the same way, Satan will do anything in his power to keep you ignorant of what God thinks.

So how can you keep your focus upon Christ when the adversary teaches people…

- to ignore God's will?
- to put self first?
- to compromise with sin?
- to fit in with the world of unbelievers?
- to water down the gospel, robbing the lost from hearing the truth?

The only way to keep your focus upon Christ is to arm yourself with the mind of Christ, living a righteous and godly life.

65 Walter B. Knight. *Knight's Treasury of 2,000 Illustrations*, p.259.

PRACTICAL ILLUSTRATIONS

12–189

PERSECUTION

1 Peter 4:12-19

(POSB, Note 1)

A By-product of Christianity

If we are walking closely with Christ, persecution should come as no surprise. In fact, it is an expected by-product of that relationship. Listen to the heart of John Wesley.

> [John Wesley] was riding along a road one day when it dawned on him that three whole days had passed in which he had suffered no persecution. Not a brick or an egg had been thrown at him for three days.
>
> Alarmed, he stopped his horse, and exclaimed, "Can it be that I have sinned, and am backslidden?"
>
> Slipping from his horse, Wesley went down on his knees and began interceding with God to show him where, if any, there had been a fault.
>
> A rough fellow on the other side of the hedge, hearing the prayer, looked across and recognized the preacher. "I'll fix that Methodist preacher," he said, picking up a brick and tossing it over at him. It missed its mark, and fell harmlessly beside John. Whereupon Wesley leaped to his feet joyfully exclaiming, "Thank God, it's all right. I still have His presence."[66]

Is your Christian walk strong enough to disturb the world? If not, maybe you need to stir the waters a little!

12–190

PERSECUTION

1 Peter 4:12-19

(POSB, Note 7)

A Character-Building Exercise

As the believer walks though the storms of persecution, he needs to continue doing good things and trusting his soul to a loving God. Here is a pointed story of the benefits of the storms that come our way.

> We were going through a great furniture factory, when our guide, the superintendent, pointed out to us a superbly grained and figured sideboard in the natural wood. "I want you to observe the beauty of this oak," he said. "It is the finest selected timber of its kind, and the secret of the intricate and beautiful graining is just this: that the trees from which it was taken grew in a spot where they were exposed to almost constant conflict with storms."
>
> What a suggestive fact! The storm-beaten tree develops the closest and finest and most intricately woven fibers. When it is cut down and the saws lay bare its exquisitely figured grain, the cabinetmaker selects it as the material for his finest work.

---

66 *J.G. Morrison.* Paul Lee Tan. *Encyclopedia of 7,700 Illustrations: Signs of the Times*, p.995.

So with the human life beset by sorrows, tests and trials. If it stands the storm, how the wind of God strengthens and beautifies it! We need life's stress. Character cannot be developed into its strongest and most beautiful forms without it.[67]

If you have never suffered persecution, you might not be as strong as you think!

12–191

PERSEVERANCE

1 Peter 5:8-9

(POSB, Intro)

Ever Guarding Against Evil

There is a story told of a lion-tamer whose reputation was known far and wide. He had a special ability to control fierce lions who drooled in anticipation of devouring him. One day, the lion-tamer died a horrible death. What happened? Did one of his lions attack him? No. He drank himself to death.

This great lion-tamer was able to control ferocious four-legged beasts. On the other hand, he was not able to control his desire for alcohol. Unable to remain sober, he was devoured by an addiction to a substance more dangerous than any animal.

Life is full of dangerous lions, the lions of terrible trials and temptations. The Christian believer is able to tame many of the dangerous lions he faces. But the danger intensifies when he slacks off and assumes everything is under control, as he indulges himself with an intoxicating worldliness. If he is not sober, he places himself in grave danger. As believers, we *must* be ever guarding against evil, always on the alert!

12–192

PRAYER

1 John 5:16-21

(POSB, Note 1)

Interceding for the Flock

God has given every believer the awesome responsibility to pray for brothers and sisters in Christ who have fallen into sin. The prayers of God's people go a long way toward restoring fellow believers entrapped by the deceit of the enemy.

A man once had a dream where he saw a field of terrified sheep encircled by a pack of angry wolves. Every time a sheep would try to break away from the circle, the wolves would immediately snap and snarl. All hope appeared to be gone as the appetite of the wolves grew more intense.

All of a sudden, a large shadow covered the field. Large eagles began to swoop down and pick up the sheep one by one, carrying them off to safety. After the man awoke, he thought to himself "What a strange dream. Lord, is there a message here from You?" The more he thought about the dream, the clearer the point became: The

67 *B.J. in Elim Evangel.* Walter B. Knight. *Knight's Master Book of 4,000 Illustrations*, pp.639-640.

eagles did not just come out of the blue, nor did they come of their own initiative. Someone knew the danger the sheep were in and sent help on their behalf. A flood of delight began to fill the man's soul. He concluded that through intercessory prayer, God would snatch backsliders up from the clutches of the wolves that would destroy them.

From that day forward, his prayers took on a whole new meaning. Each day's prayer was sure to include calling out to God on behalf of sheep straying from the fold.

Do your prayers have a specific target, or are your prayers like a shot in the dark, hoping someone, somewhere will benefit?

12–193

PRAYER

1 Peter 4:7-11

(POSB, Note 2)

Praying with Power

Alertness is key to the believer's prayer life. In order to pray effectively, the believer is charged to both pray *and* watch. Listen to this dramatic testimony of timely prayer.

In about 1949 a group of retired missionaries from China, with a few faithful praying friends, met for their regular missionary prayer meeting in Adelaide, South Australia. A great prayer burden and sense of urgency came on them as they gathered together. All felt especially burdened for Hayden Melsap, then assigned to the China Inland Mission. They unanimously decided to drop all preliminaries and go "straight to prayer." They prayed until they all felt a sense of peace and relief.

A few years later, when Hayden Melsap was on deputation in Australia, the missionaries asked him if he recalled any unusual occasion at that time. To their amazement, they found that on that day and hour Hayden and at least two other missionaries were backed against a wall in a courtyard in China, with communist guns leveled at them. Just as the officer was about to issue the command to fire, the door of the courtyard opened and a higher official entered. Shocked to see what was about to happen, he shouted, "Stop!" He then stepped up, put his arm around Melsap, and led him and others to safety.[68]

The business of the King is affected by *your* prayers. Are you being faithful to watch *and* pray?

12–194

PRIDE

1 Peter 2:4-8

(POSB, Note 3, point 3)

The Foolishness of Opposing God

Arrogance is a natural by-product of men who openly oppose God. Who would dare to attack God except a fool? Voltaire, the French agnostic, stumbled over the eternal Word of God. But God has a unique way of dealing with those who stumble on the Cornerstone.

---

68 Wesley L. Duewel. *Touch the World Through Prayer.* (Grand Rapids, MI: Francis Asbury Press, 1986), p.85.

One day Voltaire said to a friend, "It took twelve ignorant fishermen to establish Christianity; I will show the world how one Frenchman can destroy it."

Setting to his task, he openly ridiculed Sir Isaac Newton. One day Newton made a prophecy based on Dan. 12:4 and Nahum 2:4 when he said, "Man will some day be able to travel at the tremendous speed of 40 miles an hour."

Voltaire replied with, "See what a fool Christianity makes of an otherwise brilliant man, such as Sir Isaac Newton! Doesn't he know that if a man traveled 40 miles an hour, he would suffocate and his heart would stop?"

Twenty-five years after Voltaire died, his home was purchased by the Geneva Bible Society and became a Bible storage building, and his printing press was used to print an entire edition of the Bible.[69]

How ironic! The man who wanted to wipe out every trace of Christianity was foiled and indirectly became an unwilling participant in the distribution of the Word of God. A word to the wise: the Cornerstone is either a stepping stone or a crushing boulder!

12–195

PRIORITIES

1 Peter 1:22-25

(POSB, Note 3, point 2)

The Importance of Eternal Things

It has rightly been said that "you can't take it with you." As most men strive to collect things that will wither and fade away, the believer should have a much different agenda. He has an obligation to *people* not *things.* The time we spend nurturing the eternal Word of God in our own hearts and in the hearts of others will be the best investment we could ever make. Listen to one man's story of putting things in the proper perspective.

I spent a great deal of time away from home. My job demanded a lot from me, so during the first few years of my children's lives, Daddy was an absentee father. My wake-up call came the day my little daughter showed me a picture of home.

"What's that, darling?" I asked. "That's our house, Daddy," she said. Pointing to three stick figures, I asked her, "And who are these people?" Without missing a beat she said, "This one is Mommy. This one is my brother. And this one is me."

After an awkward moment of silence, I asked her "Honey, where is Daddy?" Her response broke my heart. "Daddy's not here. He's at work."

What a horrible, sinking feeling. I failed to make it into her picture of our home. I would give anything to get my stick figure in her picture.

In an act of mercy and grace, God overheard the cry of my heart. One day out of the blue, my career fell apart before my very eyes. As God began to pick up the pieces of my vocational life, little did I realize at the time that He was opening the door for a home-based business.

After a few months working at home, my daughter showed me another one of her works of art. "Daddy, look at my picture." My eye glanced at her picture and at once I saw something different—four stick figures. I asked, "Honey, who are these people?" A

---

69 *Sunday School Times.* Walter B. Knight. *3,000 Illustrations for Christian Service,* p.24.

grin that would light up the darkest room flashed across her face, "This is Mommy. This one is my brother. This one is me. And Daddy, this one is you playing with me!"

Building relationships with others in the family of God is infinitely more important than accumulating any amount of wealth. When the family photo is taken, make sure you are in the picture!

12–196

PROSPERITY

3 John 1-8

(POSB, Note 2, point 2)

The True Measure of Success

A common misconception is that prosperity applies only to material wealth. But God's standards are much higher and much purer.

An old man showed up at the back door of the house we were renting. Opening the door a few cautious inches, we saw his eyes were glassy and his furrowed face glistened with silver stubble. He clutched a wicker basket holding a few unappealing vegetables. He bid us good morning and offered his produce for sale. We were uneasy enough to make a quick purchase to alleviate both our pity and our fear.

To our chagrin, he returned the next week, introducing himself as Mr. Roth, the man who lived in the shack down [the] road. As our fears subsided, we got close enough to realize that it wasn't alcohol, but cataracts, that marbleized his eyes. On subsequent visits, he would shuffle in, wearing two mismatched right shoes, and pull out a harmonica. With glazed eyes set on a future glory, he'd puff out old gospel tunes between conversations about vegetables and religion.

On one visit, he exclaimed, "The Lord is so good! I came out of my shack this morning and found a bag full of shoes and clothing on my porch."

"That's wonderful, Mr. Roth," we said. "We're happy for you."

"You know what's even more wonderful?" he asked. "Just yesterday I met some people that could use them."[70]

12–197

PURE - PURITY

1 Peter 1:22-25

(POSB, Note 1)

Caring for Those You Love

With a little common sense, the *common* cold is fairly simple to control. But how about sin? If we are not pure in heart, we are quite capable of infecting others. Listen to this lesson from history as it applies to spiritual hygiene.

In 1818, Ignaz Phillip Semmelweis was born into a world of dying women. The finest hospitals lost one out of six young dying mothers to the scourge of "childbed fever."

---

70 Alice Gray. *More Stories for the Heart*, p. 45.

A doctor's daily routine began in the dissecting room where he performed autopsies. From there he made his way to the hospital to examine expectant mothers without ever pausing to wash his hands. Dr. Semmelweis was the first man in history to associate such examinations with the resultant infection and death. His own practice was to wash with a chlorine solution, and after eleven years and the delivery of 8,537 babies, he lost only 184 mothers—about one in fifty.

He spent the vigor of his life lecturing and debating with his colleagues. Once he argued, "Puerperal fever is caused by decomposed material conveyed to a wound...I have shown how it can be prevented. I have proved all that I have said. But while we talk, talk, talk, gentlemen, women are dying. I am not asking anything world shaking. I am asking you only to wash...For God's sake, wash your hands."

But virtually no one believed him. Doctors and midwives had been delivering babies for thousands of years without washing, and no outspoken Hungarian was going to change them now! Semmelweis died insane at the age of 47, his wash basins discarded, his colleagues laughing in his face, and the death rattle of a thousand women ringing in his ears.

"Wash me!" was the anguished prayer of King David. "Wash!" was the message of John the Baptist. "Unless I wash you, you have no part with me," said the towel-draped Jesus to Peter. Without our being washed clean, we all die from the contamination of sin. For God's sake, wash!"[71]

Cleanliness is important for many reasons—not the least of which is loving others and caring about their well-being. How much more vital is it that we keep spiritually pure?

12–198

REPENTANCE

1 Peter 2:21-25

(POSB, Note 3, point 2)

How to Be Debt Free

Repentance is the only way to the Father. All of us are sheep who have gone astray according to our own fallen will. It is God's will that we turn to the Shepherd of our souls, the Lord Jesus Christ. Listen to this striking story on the power of repentance.

Governor Neff, of Texas, spoke to the assembled convicts of a penitentiary of that state. He finished by saying that he would remain to listen if any man wanted to speak with him. He further announced that what he heard would be held in confidence....

When the meeting was over, a large group of men remained, many of them lifetermers. One by one they each told the governor that [they were] there through a frame-up, an injustice, a judicial blunder; each asked that [they] be freed. Finally, one man came up and said, "Mr. Governor, I just want to say that I am guilty"....This man the governor pardoned. So must it be with the great God who alone can pardon.[72]

Admitting to and repenting of our sins will pay eternal rewards!

71 Craig B. Larson, Editor. *Illustrations for Preaching & Teaching*, p.206.

72 Donald Grey Barnhouse. *Let Me Illustrate*, p.262.

Practical Illustrations

12–199

Respect

1 Peter 1:17-21

(POSB, Note 1)

Showing Proper Reverence

Respect is quickly becoming a faint memory in many cultures today. Unfortunately, this lack of respect has even found a way into the church.

> One day two men were talking while eating lunch. The first man said to the other, "I notice you've got a bumper-sticker on your car that reads 'Heaven Bound.' Are you a Christian?" "Oh, yea," said the second man. "I really owe a lot to the man upstairs. He's my good buddy in the sky."
>
> The first man paused for a moment, then asked, "Well, what about your front license plate—'Hell on Wheels'? What does that have to do with being a Christian?" The second man was quickly convicted by the Holy Spirit. It sounded like his car was going to heaven while he was going to hell. He had made the mistake of being too flippant with his faith. God was not his good buddy. God was his Almighty heavenly Father. The man owed God much more respect than he had been giving.

Neither is God *our* good buddy. God is *our* Almighty heavenly Father. And let's be honest—we all owe God much more respect than we give Him.

12–200

Resurrection

1 Peter 1:17-21

(POSB, Note 5)

Only God Can Give Life

Only God has the ability to raise men from the dead. Try as he may, man is powerless to do the same. Listen closely to this example in futility:

> A man named Brown was hanged in Philadelphia some time ago. In ten minutes after he was legally dead he was resting on a table in the ... laboratory. Around the table were three of the most famous physiologists of the scientific world. Could motion and life be restored to that inanimate body? Science waited anxiously for an answer to the question.
>
> A sharp wire, charged with electricity, was applied to the various nerve centers of the body and brain. A superstitious layman would have been horrified at the result. Brown raised first his right hand and then his left. His head moved. His mouth twitched in a convulsive grin. The cords of his neck swelled and the mouth opened as if he would complete his unfinished sentence on the scaffold. The hands drew up and then extended. Unceasingly the electric wire prodded center after center in the nervous organism. At a fresh touch from the plying needle the body sat upright. There seemed to be breath, for the respiratory organs were agitated. Would he walk? Would he talk?
>
> Science was anxious; another stroke and it had found the secret of life. But placed on the floor, the body fell over limp—dead. Science had demonstrated wonders, but had failed to raise the dead.[73]

---

73 *S.T. Nicholls.* Paul Lee Tan. *Encyclopedia of 7,700 Illustrations: Signs of the Times*, p.1144.

Practical Illustrations

Jesus said,

> **"I am the resurrection, and the life: he that believeth in me, though he were dead, yet shall he live" (Jn. 11:25).**

12–201

The Return of Christ

1 Peter 3:15-18

(POSB, intro)

Ready and Waiting

Have you ever waited for someone to meet you at a restaurant...and waited...and waited? As you glanced at your watch and cut your eye toward the entrance, the waiting seemed interminable. In the end, did you get tired of waiting and leave, or did you patiently wait for your party to join you? Every day we miss important and unique opportunities because we are unwilling to wait a moment longer. Think of all the...

- occasions to learn
- times of laughter
- rich moments of fellowship
- opportunities to witness

...that are missed due to our impatience. Think of the time that is spent fussing and fuming instead of praying and meditating—all because we run out of patience. Relative to these examples is a far greater reason for waiting. God has charged each believer to live in an expectant frame of mind, waiting for the Lord's return.

But as you wait for His call to move out, to move on to heaven, be certain you are still living and watching and growing in the Lord—ever showing others the way to salvation.

12–202

Righteousness

1 John 1:10-2:2

(POSB, Note 1)

Owning Up to the Truth

God's Word states that every person is a sinner in need of a Savior. If a person does not accept the fact that he is a sinner, he cannot be saved. It is that simple.

> The story is told of a slick politician who was present at a high dollar social event. As he stood in the grand lobby of the mansion, he was trying to get campaign support from a couple of wealthy donors. The politician was new in the area and had not prepared himself for the event, but he reasoned that he could always count on his quick wit and brash humor.
>
> As the politician finished speaking with potential supporters, he turned to view the crowd. Just then, two ladies descended the beautiful spiral staircase. "That is one ugly woman," he mumbled under his breath.

One of the men he had just been speaking with wheeled around and angrily replied, "That's my wife!" "Uh, the other one," the politician quickly muttered. "That's my daughter!" the husband retorted with an icy glare. The politician thought for a split second, looked the man squarely in the eye, then innocently remarked, "What? I didn't say anything."—SOURCE UNKNOWN

Needless to say, that politician didn't get elected commissioner. But then some people will try anything to avoid looking guilty. However, admitting our guilt and sin to the Lord is *required* if we are to be forgiven. Denying it won't help. We must agree with God's Word. We are all sinners in need of a Savior.

12–203

RIGHTEOUSNESS

1 John 2:28-29

(POSB, Note 3)

The Power to Live Righteously

A truly righteous life is a life that abides in Christ, *knowing* that only Jesus Christ can provide all the believer needs to live.

A young boy doing his best to lift a suitcase twice his size strained and grunted in an effort to pick up the huge bag, but to no avail. He could not budge it. After several moments, his father walked into the room and saw his son struggling. "Having some trouble with that, son?" the father asked. With a long face turned several shades of red, the young lad replied, "Yes, I've tried to push it and pull it and it just won't move."

Seeing an opportunity to teach a valuable lesson, the father pressed on, "Are you sure you've tried everything?" The exasperated boy looked up at his father and said, "Daddy, I've thought of everything. I'm out of ideas and I'm out of strength."

His father then placed his large hand on the young boy's head and said, "Son, you've forgotten one thing that can help you move this heavy suitcase. You've forgotten about me. You can always call on me."

In the same sense, the only way we as believers can live righteous lives is with the help of our Heavenly Father. Any attempt to live the Christian life without God's help is like trying to move an unmovable weight. Our righteousness is like filthy rags that weigh us down. But Christ's righteousness sets us free, free to tackle the impossible!

12–204

SALVATION

1 John 3:4-9

(POSB, Note 2)

Acknowledging Your Sin and Your Savior

In a wonderful act of love, humility, and sacrifice, Jesus left His home in glory in order to save man from the muck and mire of sin. Can you identify with the following story?

A so-called higher critic spoke scornfully of the Bible story of man's creation. With a grin on his face he said, "Think of God taking a piece of mud in hand, breathing on it, and charging it into a man!"

In the audience was a man who had sunken low into the muck of sin, but who was now transformed by the wondrous grace of God. He stood fearlessly to his feet and said to the critic of God's Word: "I will not discuss the creation of man with you, but I will tell you this: God stooped down and picked up the dirtiest bit of mud in our town. He breathed upon it by His Spirit. It was newly created. It was changed from a wicked wretch into a man who now hates his former sins and loves the God who saved him. *I was that bit of mud!*"[74]

This man boldly acknowledged his sin and his Savior—an absolutely essential step for every one of us!

12–205

SALVATION

1 John 5:6-8

(POSB, Note 4, point 3)

Falling into His Grace

The only way a man can live forever with God is to believe that Jesus Christ is the Son of God. Can you trust the testimonies you have heard and read? Listen closely to this captivating story.

A traveler upon a lonely road was set upon by bandits who robbed him of his all. They then led him into the depths of the forest. There, in the darkness, they tied a rope to the limb of a great tree, and [forced] him [to] catch hold of the end of it. Swinging him out into the blackness of surrounding space, they told him he was hanging over the brink of an [unsteady]...precipice.

The moment he let go he would be dashed to pieces on the rocks below. And then they left him. His soul was filled with horror at the awful doom impending. He clutched despairingly the end of the swaying rope. But each dreadful moment only made his fate more sure. His strength steadily failed. At last he could hold on no longer. The end had come. His clenched fingers relaxed their...grip. He fell—*six inches*, to the solid earth at his feet! It was only a ruse of the robbers to gain time in escaping. And when he let go it was not to death, but to the safety which had been waiting him through all his time of terror.

Friend, clutching will not save you. It is only Satan's trick to keep you from *being* saved. And all the while is your heart not full of fear? Let go!...Underneath is—Jesus![75]

You can believe all the witnesses you have heard—Jesus Christ *is* the Son of God. Jesus Christ *did* come to earth to die for you and save you from your sins. Now, as the saying goes, "Let go (of your sins) and let God (save you)."

---

74 Walter B. Knight. *Knight's Treasury of 2,000 Illustrations*, p.341.

75 *James McConkey*. Walter B. Knight. *Knight's Treasury of 2,000 Illustrations*, pp.341-342.

12–206

SALVATION

1 John 3:4-9

(POSB, Note 5)

Freed from a Life of Sin

Salvation is too exciting to be taken for granted. But freedom can never be fully appreciated unless a person thinks of the bondage he has escaped.

> During a Texas revival meeting led by Mordecai Ham, a man in the congregation was overcome by the love and mercy of God. He had killed four men and never dreamed God could care for him. This man was so touched by the gospel that he stood up during that revival in 1910 and shouted, "Saved! Saved! Saved!" Jack Scofield, the musician for the revival, was so moved by this joyful outburst that he used those words to write that popular hymn [Saved! Saved! Saved!] the next afternoon. The inspiration for this widely sung hymn came from the enthusiastic gratitude of a four-time murderer who found the grace of God.[76]

Saved! Have you claimed God's exciting promise of salvation and freedom for yourself?

12–207

SALVATION

1 Peter 1:10-12

(POSB, Note 7)

God's Wondrous Plan of Salvation

Christ paid the ultimate price to bring God's wondrous plan of salvation to the world. This is the most important fact in all of history. Bill Hybels illustrates:

> I was emotionally moved as I sat in my study and watched this young soldier on a television newscast. He seemed almost unaware of the TV reporter who was intruding into his private moment of contemplation and relived memories.
>
> They were at the Vietnam Veteran's Memorial in Washington, D.C. The soldier was by the black granite wall, which is etched with the names of all the Americans who lost their lives in the Vietnam War.
>
> He just stood there, tearfully staring at the wall and tracing his finger over the letters of another soldier's name engraved there. He never even looked at the reporter of the camera, but you could feel his pain. "He gave his life for me," was all he whispered as he kept moving his finger across the friend's name.
>
> As I sat there feeling a small dose of what this soldier must have been experiencing, it struck me that he would be affected for the rest of his life because someone had been willing to sacrifice everything for him.[77]

We, too, should stand in stark amazement at the fact that Jesus Christ came in the flesh and died on the cross to save us from our sins.

---

76 *Leadership Journal.* (Carol Stream, IL: *Christianity Today*, Fall 1988), p.33.

77 Bill Hybels and Mark Mittleberg. *Becoming a Contagious Christian.* (Grand Rapids, MI: Zondervan Publishing House, 1994), p. 81.

12–208

SALVATION

2 Peter 1:16-21

(POSB, Note 1, point 1)

The Greatness of Christ

What kind of Savior do you need? In a lost and dying world, He must be all-powerful!

This story is told of Daniel Webster when he was in the prime of his manhood. He was dining in the company of literary men in Boston. During the dinner the conversation turned [to] the subject of Christianity. Mr. Webster frankly stated his belief in the divinity of Christ and his dependence upon the atonement of the Saviour.

One said to him, "Mr. Webster, can you comprehend how Christ could be both God and man?" Mr. Webster promptly replied, "No, sir, I cannot comprehend it. If I could comprehend him, he would be no greater than myself. I feel that I need a super-human Saviour."[78]

If your god is small enough to comprehend, then he's not great enough to be your Savior. Like Webster, we all need a "super-human Saviour"—the Lord Jesus Christ.

12–209

SALVATION

1 Peter 2:9-10

(POSB, Note 2)

Opening the Floodgates of Praise

Man is so lost that he can never save himself. But God has done through Jesus Christ what no man can do for himself. In a world infested with sin, Christ reached down and rescued sinners who had no hope. This is the glorious message of the gospel. Once the believer understands all that God has done for him, a sincere gratitude is the only appropriate response.

The following drama was originally reported by Peter Michelmore in the October 1987 *Reader's Digest*:

Normally the flight from Nassau to Miami took Walter Wyatt, Jr., only sixty-five minutes. But on December 5, 1986, he attempted it after thieves had looted the navigational equipment in his Beechcraft. With only a compass and a hand-held radio, Walter flew into skies blackened by storm clouds.

When his compass began to gyrate, Walter concluded he was headed in the wrong direction. He flew his plane below the clouds, hoping to spot something, but soon he knew he was lost. He put out a mayday call, which brought a Coast Guard Falcon search plane to lead him to an emergency landing strip only six miles away.

Suddenly Wyatt's right engine coughed its last and died. The fuel tank had run dry. Around 8 P.M. Wyatt could do little more than glide the plane into the water. Wyatt survived the crash, but his plane disappeared quickly, leaving him bobbing on the water in a leaky life vest.

---

78 *Christian Witness.* Paul Lee Tan. *Encyclopedia of 7,700 Illustrations: Signs of the Times*, p.649.

With blood on his forehead, Wyatt floated on his back. Suddenly he felt a hard bump against his body. A shark had found him. Wyatt kicked the intruder and wondered if he would survive the night. He managed to stay afloat for the next ten hours.

In the next morning, Wyatt saw no airplanes, but in the water a dorsal fin was headed for him. Twisting, he felt the hide of a shark brush against him. In a moment, two more bull sharks sliced through the water toward him. Again he kicked the sharks, and they veered away, but he was nearing exhaustion.

Then he heard the hum of a distant aircraft. When it was within a half mile, he waved his orange vest. The pilot dropped a smoke canister and radioed the cutter Cape York, which was twelve minutes away: "Get moving, cutter! There's a shark targeting this guy!"

As the Cape York pulled alongside Wyatt, a Jacob's ladder was dropped over the side. Wyatt climbed wearily out of the water and onto the ship, where he fell to his knees and kissed the deck.

He'd been saved. He didn't need encouragement or better techniques. Nothing less than outside intervention could have rescued him from sure death. How much we are like Walter Wyatt![79]

What else can you do but praise God's Holy Name for saving you?

12–210

SERVICE

3 John 1-8

Investing Wisely in Others

(POSB, Note 4, point 2)

For thousands of years, God has used the home for a place of ministry. After all, before church buildings were built, God's people gathered in each other's homes for worship and fellowship.

Years ago a married couple had a tremendous burden for the young people of their community. For many of the youth, drugs and sex had become a way of life. The couple saw that the only way to fill the empty lives of these young people was to fill them with Jesus.

The couple opened up their home, anticipating a handful of kids might come. But they were overwhelmed when over fifty love-starved youth crammed into their living room. Like baby birds in a nest, they came expecting to be fed every week. In that living room, eternal life was received. The power of drugs and sex was broken. And for the first time in their lives, these kids finally had a purpose: to love God, to help their friends and classmates find Christ and the fullness of life and joy in Him.

The fruit of this Christian couple's ministry is still going on.

Did this couple have to make any sacrifices? Sure. They sacrificed their time and the wear and tear on their home. Years later they replaced the worn-out sofa and the carpet. But it was a good investment: changed lives for a changed sofa and carpet. It's never too early—and never too late—to start investing in the lives of others!

---

79 Craig B. Larson, Editor. *Illustrations for Preaching & Teaching*, pp.203-204.

Practical Illustrations

12–211

Service

1 Peter 5:1-4

(POSB, Note 2, point 1)

The Need to Serve Willingly

Securing new church workers is a never-ending job. Pastor and author Bill Hybels pokes fun at the annual recruiting task.

> It's August. Throughout the country, the late summer ritual begins. And it's not a pretty sight.
>
> Pastor Bob has just received his annual flood of resignation notes. Sunday school teachers, ushers, Bible study leaders, youth leaders, and assorted other "servers" have called it quits. He's not surprised. It happens every year. Some people offer lengthy explanations. Others say simply, "I've done my part."
>
> Now Pastor Bob knows that the ministries of the church can't continue unless someone fills all these empty positions. So, with unprecedented determination, he begins psyching up for the annual "August Recruitment Campaign."
>
> Pastor Bob isn't the first to fight this battle. His predecessor fought it, too. In fact, it's become somewhat of a tradition—one that even his most tradition-bound congregants would like to do without. So, while Pastor Bob is psyching himself up, his two hundred members are doing the same. They know they'll have to be tough to resist this year's recruitment campaign. It's going to be war!...
>
> Pastor Bob does know how much resistance has surfaced in his congregation. So this year he's bringing out the heavy artillery. He's planning a four-sided series called "Serve or Burn." Every week he'll use a dramatic illustration from *Foxe's Book of Martyrs*. There's nothing like true-to-life stories of people who gave up their lives for serving Christ...
>
> On the fourth week, he'll bring out his secret weapon. Seven-year-old Suzi Miller. He'll cradle the little darling on his lap and ask her what it will be like to spend a whole year in second grade Sunday school with no teacher.
>
> He hopes against hope that she'll cry. If she does, he'll win the war hands down. Sure as shootin' he'll win the war.
>
> So the stage is set. It's going to be an interesting August.[80]

Members of the church should serve willingly, lovingly, not out of guilt or threat of humiliation. Are you doing your part?

12–212

Sin

1 Peter 2:1-3

(POSB, Note 1, point 5)

Adopting a Zero-Tolerance Policy

We must have an aggressive attitude when it comes to fighting sin. Evangelist Billy Sunday was a man who declared war on whatever sin he found in his life.

---

80 Bill Hybels. *Honest To God?* (Grand Rapids, MI: Zondervan Publishing House, 1990), pp.107-108.

Billy Sunday, the baseball evangelist and reformer, never spared himself nor those he wanted to help in the vigor of his attacks on sin. He thundered against evil from the Gay Nineties through the Great Depression. He preached Christ as the only answer to man's needs until his death in 1935.

"I'm against sin," he said. "I'll kick it as long as I've got a foot, and I'll fight it as long as I've got a fist. I'll butt it as long as I've got a head. I'll bite it as long as I've got a tooth. When I'm old and fistless and footless and toothless, I'll gum it till I go home to Glory and it goes home to perdition!"[81]

Do you hate sin...enough to fight it passionately?

12–213

SIN

1 John 1:8-9

(POSB, Note 1)

Confession Is Good for the Soul

A lot of people have difficulty admitting that they are sinners. Mrs. Smith, an elderly woman, was highly offended at the suggestion. Here is her story.

An elder at a big church went to visit Mrs. Smith in her home. After a friendly conversation, he shocked her by asking, "Mrs. Smith, are you a sinner?" "Sir, how dare you," she replied indignantly. "Why, I'll have you know I am a charter member of the church. I have sung in the choir and have served as president of the ladies' auxiliary. I am a good citizen and a good person."

Unphased, the elder pressed on. "But have you ever sinned?" He then opened the Bible on her table to 1 John 1:9 and read: "If we confess our sins, he is faithful and just to forgive us our sins, and to cleanse us from all unrighteousness."

After reading, the elder pointedly asked, "Mrs. Smith, the Bible says Jesus came to save sinners. Has He come to save you?"

For the first time in her life, Mrs. Smith realized that all her good works would not save her. She needed God's saving grace. "Do you think God would still save an old woman like me?" she asked him. The elder took her by the hand and led her in a prayer of repentance as her name was written in the Lamb's Book of Life.

Jesus did not die for perfect people. He died for sinners ... just like you.

12–214

SIN

1 John 5:16-21

(POSB, Note 3)

Dropping a Few Pounds

A person must first realize that this world is under the power of Satan before he can realize his need to be free from sin. Satan has contaminated the world with a highly infectious disease called sin. So be careful what

81 Paul Lee Tan. *Encyclopedia of 7,700 Illustrations: Signs of the Times*, p.1283.

you touch. Don't pick up anything from the world that might weigh you down.

> [D. L. Moody] did not appear on the platform as usual at the beginning of the service, but had Mr. Sankey [his song leader] to say, "Mr. Moody will come onto the platform looking different than you ever saw him at the preaching hour."
>
> With their curiosity sufficiently piqued and the time for the sermon at hand, Mr. Moody appeared with a tremendous pack strapped onto his shoulder. He walked slowly across the platform, turned, and walked back. Then he asked the audience, "Do you think I could preach like Jesus wants me to preach with this load on my back? ... There is no whiskey bottle nor a pair of dice in it. It is made up of clothes and many other harmless things. [But] some of you are trying to serve Christ while you carry a lot of 'weights' on your back. Jesus said that you must be different, 'separated' from the world. You must leave some otherwise harmless things beyond."[82]

What in the world is weighing you down?

12–215

SPIRITUAL WARFARE

1 John 2:12–24

(POSB, Note 1, point 3)

Living On a Higher Plane

An important pillar in the believer's life is remembering *what* he has overcome. Spiritual maturity carries the distinctive mark of a loving relationship with God. James Decanter notes a moving example:

> My wife, Peggy, and I were on a World Missions tour visiting Haiti. For three days we had seen unbelievable poverty. Children with no clothing, families with no homes—not even a shelter. The hollow look of the faces...was a look of utter hopelessness.
>
> [But] there was a noticeable exception. The people of God! Even though most of them were also poor, they had smiles on their faces and purpose in their hearts. It was evident they were citizens of another country.
>
> Wednesday night our group attended worship....We arrived about 15 minutes before scheduled service time, but they were already joyously worshipping God. The building was packed beyond intended capacity. Although we did not understand their language, we recognized the old song they were singing, "No One Ever Cared for Me Like Jesus." We were overwhelmed with the intensity of their worship, the pouring out of their hearts to God, the obvious loving relationship they had with God. A big lump came in my throat, and Peggy began to weep. One of the Haitian ladies, apparently thinking we did not understand how to worship, tapped Peggy on the shoulder and in broken English instructed, "No cry. Clap!"
>
> We were so moved by their worship because for three days we had seen poverty, hunger, and desperation on every hand. It was their relationship with God that lifted them higher than life's conditions. They were living on a higher plane.[83]

---

82 Walter B. Knight. *Knight's Master Book of 4,000 Illustrations*, p.749.

83 Robert White. *Life in the Spirit.* (Minsk, Belarus: Spirit Life Books, 2000), p. 84.

12–216

SPIRITUAL WARFARE

1 Peter 5:8-9

Ready, Willing, and Able

(POSB, Note 1, point 2)

The believer simply cannot ignore this one fact: the devil *will* attack, wherever and whenever he can. No one is exempt. Preparation for battle is the only sensible option.

> At the battle of Gettysburg, a general reported to Longstreet, the commanding officer, that he could not bring his men up again. Longstreet answered sarcastically, "Very well; never mind, then; just let them stay where they are; the enemy's going to advance, and that will spare you the trouble."[84]

Be ready. Spiritual battles will come. As Jesus said,

> **"In the world ye shall have tribulation: but be of good cheer; I have overcome the world" (John 16:33).**

12–217

SPIRITUAL WARFARE

1 Peter 5:8-9

Relying on God's Strength

(POSB, Note 3, point 2)

It is impossible to resist the devil in our own strength. If we do attempt it on our own, our strength is quickly exhausted. The key to resisting Satan is to force him to deal with the One who lives in our heart.

> Martin Luther was often very graphic in his description of the activities of the Devil. Asked one time how he overcame the Devil, he replied, "Well, when he comes knocking upon the door of my heart, and asks 'Who lives here?' the dear Lord Jesus goes to the door and says, 'Martin Luther used to live here but he has moved out. Now I live here.' The Devil seeing the nail-prints in the hands, and the pierced side, takes flight immediately."
>
> It is surely good for every life and for every home to have Jesus as a permanent resident. This assured, heavenly blessings are sure to fall upon such bodies.[85]

When Satan knocks, who opens the door of your heart?

84 *Current Anecdotes.* Paul Lee Tan. *Encyclopedia of 7,700 Illustrations: Signs of the Times*, p.1444.

85 *Sword of the Lord.* Walter B. Knight. *Knight's Master Book of 4,000 Illustrations*, p.167.

PRACTICAL ILLUSTRATIONS

12–218

SUBMISSION

1 Peter 2:13-17

(POSB, Note 1, point 1)

The Protection of God

God requires us (believers) to place our trust in Him as we submit to earthly authorities. He promises to protect us from harm if we will trust Him and obey the laws of the land. Max Lucado humorously illustrates.

> My route to the office takes me south to an intersection where I and every other person in Texas turn east. Each morning I wait long minutes in a long line at long light, always mumbling, "There must be a better way." A few days back I found it. While still a half-mile from the light, I spotted a shortcut, an alley behind a shopping center. It was worth a try. I turned on my blinker, made a quick left, bid farewell to the crawling commuters, and took my chances. I weaved in between the dumpsters and over the speed bumps and ... it worked! The alley led me to my eastbound avenue several minutes faster than the rest of society.
>
> Lewis and Clark would have been proud. I certainly was. From then on, I was ahead of the pack. Every morning while the rest of the cars waited in line, I veered onto my private autobahn and smugly applauded myself for seeing what others missed.
>
> One morning Denalyn was with me in the car. "I'm about to remind you why you married me," I told her as we drew near to the intersection. "See that long line of cars? Hear that dirge from the suburbs? See that humdrum of humanity? It's not for me. Hang on!"
>
> Like a hunter on a safari, I swerved from the six-lane onto the one-lane and shared with my sweetheart my secret expressway to freedom. "What do you think?" I asked her, awaiting her worship.
>
> "I think you broke the law."
>
> "What?"
>
> "You just went the wrong way on a one-way street."
>
> I did. She was right. Somehow I'd missed the sign....
>
> My problem is not what I did before I knew the law. My problem is what I want to do now, after I know the law. You'd think that I would have no desire to use the alley, but I do!
>
> ...My "ought to" says, "It's illegal."
>
> My "want to" answers, "But I've never been caught."
>
> My "ought to" reminds [me], "The law is the law."[86]

Submission to authority is not only best—it is what God commands!

12–219

SUFFERING

1 Peter 2:21-25

(POSB, Note 1)

The Mark of a Genuine Christian

The road of righteousness leads *through* the Cross. Just check the map. Suffering and persecution are on the way.

---

86 Max Lucado. *In the Grip of Grace.* (Dallas, TX: Word Publishing, 1996), pp.139-141.

A Spirit-filled worker connected with the African Inland Mission was giving his testimony after returning from a very dangerous service in the World War. He said that if someone sent him on a journey and told him the road to take, warning him that at a certain point he would come to a dangerous crossing of the river, at another point to a forest infested with wild beasts, he would come to that dangerous river crossing with the satisfaction of knowing that he was on the right road. So he told them that the Lord had predicted that Christians would have tribulation, and when the tribulations came he knew he was on the right road.[87]

Troubles in this world are to be expected. As someone once wisely said, "The true believer doesn't complain about the thorns; he just praises God that He loves us enough to put beautiful roses on the top of every stem."

12–220

TESTIMONY

3 John 9-14

(POSB, Note 2, point 3)

Always Being Watched

If you are a leader...

- in the home
- in the workplace
- in the church

... or in any public place, your life will be closely examined. People will be looking to you for your reactions toward life experiences.

A minister was making a wooden trellis to support a climbing vine. As he was pounding away, he noticed that a little boy was watching him. The youngster didn't say a word, so the preacher kept on working, thinking the lad would leave. But he didn't. Pleased at the thought that his work was being admired, the pastor said, "Well, son, trying to pick up some pointers on gardening?"

"No," replied the boy, "I'm just waiting to hear what a preacher says when he hits his thumb with a hammer."[88]

A life that is rooted and grounded in Christ will always respond in a positive way...even when the trials of life hit.

12–221

TRIALS

1 Peter 1:6-9

(POSB, Note 1, point 2)

Gathering Your Strength

Have you ever wondered why your trials have to be so hard? Wouldn't it make more sense for God to go easy on you? God allows trials to come to His children for a very specific purpose. This is illustrated by Gary

87 *Sunday School Times.* Walter B. Knight. *3,000 Illustrations for Christian Service*, p.636.

88 Michael P. Green. *Illustrations for Biblical Preaching*, p.399.

Richmond as he describes the birth of a giraffe from his book, *A View from the Zoo.*

The first thing to emerge are the baby giraffe's front hooves and head. A few minutes later the plucky newborn is hurled forth, falls ten feet, and lands on its back. Within seconds, he rolls to an upright position with his legs tucked under his body. From this position he considers the world for the first time and shakes off the last vestiges of the birthing fluid from his eyes and ears.

The mother giraffe lowers her head long enough to take a quick look. Then she positions herself directly over her calf. She waits for about a minute, and then she does the most unreasonable thing. She swings her long, pendulous leg outward and kicks her baby, so that it is sent sprawling head over heals. [heels].

When it doesn't get up, the violent process is repeated over and over again. The struggle to rise is momentous. As the baby calf grows tired, the mother kicks it again to stimulate its efforts....Finally, the calf stands for the first time on its wobbly legs.

Then the mother giraffe does the most remarkable thing. She kicks it off its feet again. Why? She wants it to remember how it got up. In the wild, baby giraffes must be able to get up as quickly as possible to stay with the herd, where there is safety. Lions, hyenas, leopards, and wild hunting dogs all enjoy young giraffes, and they'd get it too, if the mother didn't teach her calf to get up quickly and get with it....

I've thought about the birth of the giraffe many times. I can see its parallel in my own life. There have been many times when it seemed that I had just stood up after a trial, only to be knocked down again by the next. It was God helping me to remember how it was that I got up, urging me always to walk with him, in his shadow, under his care.[89]

When the trials of life knock you down, reach out to the One who is always there to pick you up again.

12–222

TRIALS

1 Peter 1:6-9

(POSB, Note 2, point 2)

In All Things Give Thanks

Though painful, a difficult trial is a precious gift from God. It is during the difficult times that we really get to know God's love. Therefore, a trial should never be regretted or scorned, but learned from. Experiencing the storms of life are a crucial part of the growing process.

An elderly man asked a boy to go with him into the woods to cut down some hickory trees to make ax handles. They soon came to several young hickory trees. The boy said, "These trees would make good ax handles. Let's cut them down."

The old man said, "These trees in the lowlands have been protected from the storms which rage higher up. Let's go to the heights where the trees have been rocked

89 Craig B. Larson. *Illustrations for Preaching and Teaching,* p. 265.

back and forth by fierce winds. Those trees have been hardened by the tempest and they will make much stronger ax handles!"[90]

Only God knows how to prepare His children for service. Will you thank Him even *during* the storms of life?

12–223

TRUTH

1 John 5:9-15

(POSB, intro)

Facing the Facts

God has declared His Son to be the Source of eternal life. Denying the facts will not change the truth.

An old story tells of a desert nomad who awakened hungry in the middle of the night. He lit a candle and began eating dates from a bowl beside his bed. He took a bite from one end and saw a worm in it, so he threw it out of the tent. He bit into the second date, found another worm, and threw it away also. Reasoning that he wouldn't have any dates left to eat if he continued, he blew out the candle and quickly ate all the dates.

Many there are who prefer darkness and denial to the light of reality.[91]

12–224

UNITY

1 Peter 3:8-9

(POSB, Note 1, point 4)

Supporting One Another

The great challenge for the believer is to subject his mind to the mind of Christ. It is both unhealthy and unnatural for a body to have more than one mind. But if everyone is thinking alike—focused upon Jesus Christ and His mission—then everyone grows.

The article "What Good is a Tree?" in *Reader's Digest* explained that when the roots of trees touch, there is a substance that reduces competition. In fact, this unknown fungus helps link roots of different trees—even of dissimilar species. A whole forest may be linked together. If one tree has access to water, another to nutrients, and a third to sunlight, the trees have the means to share with one another.

Like trees in a forest, Christians in the church need and support one another.[92]

Having one mind, the mind of Christ, is the only way to achieve peace and unity. It is also the only way to carry out the ministry of Christ.

90 Walter B. Knight. *Knight's Treasury of 2,000 Illustrations*, p. 403.

91 Craig B. Larson, Editor. *Illustrations for Preaching and Teaching*, p.59.

92 Ibid., p.32.

PRACTICAL ILLUSTRATIONS

12–225

WITNESS–WITNESSING

Jude 17-25

(POSB, Note 3, point 2)

Caring Enough to Share

Do you know people who are victims of false teaching? Have you ever confronted them about the eventual destination of their soul? Sometimes we tend to be too careful, afraid of offending those who are lost. But the truth is striking: they have already been offended by the message of the cross of Christ. Christian love and compassion should compel us to share the gospel with the lost. How will they know unless we tell them?

> Dwight L. Moody once saw a man freezing to death on the street in Chicago. Moody could not just talk this man into warmth. He pounded him with his fist and got him really angry. The man began to pound back and then got up and ran after Moody. That got his blood circulating and saved his life. Our loud and outspoken witnessing may make people angry, but at least it may awaken them from their spiritual stupor.[93]

Who needs your boldness, your compassion today?

12–226

WITNESS–WITNESSING

1 Peter 3:13-17

(POSB, Note 3, point 3)

Doing What We Can

Every believer has the God-given responsibility to share the gospel with others. We may not all be evangelists, but Christ has given us a story to tell. Rusty Stevens, a director for the Navigators, shares his story.

> As I feverishly pushed the lawn mower around our yard, I wondered if I'd finish before dinner. Mikey, our 6-year-old, walked up and, without even asking, stepped in front of me and placed his hands on the mower handle. Knowing that he wanted to help me, I quit pushing.
>
> The mower quickly slowed to a stop. Chuckling inwardly at his struggles, I resisted the urge to say, "Get out of here, kid. You're in my way." and said instead, "Here, Son. I'll help you." As I resumed pushing, I bowed my head back and leaned forward, and walked spread-legged to avoid colliding with Mikey. The grass cutting continued, but more slowly, and less efficiently than before, because Mikey was "helping" me.
>
> Suddenly, tears came to my eyes as it hit me: "This is the way my heavenly Father allows me to *help* him build his kingdom!" I pictured my heavenly Father at work seeking, saving, and transforming the lost, and there I was, with my weak hands "*helping*." My Father could do the work by himself, but he doesn't. He chooses to stoop gracefully to allow me to co-labor with him. Why? For *my* sake, because he wants me to have the privilege of ministering with him.[94]

The opportunity is there. God is there waiting to help you. What are you waiting for?

---

93 *Power.* Walter B. Knight. *Knight's Master Book of 4,000 Illustrations*, p.72.

94 Craig B. Larson, Editor. *Illustrations for Preaching & Teaching*, p.153.

12–227

WITNESS–WITNESSING

2 Peter 3:11-14

Evidence You Can Depend Upon

(POSB, Note 1, point 2)

Do you live a holy and godly life? As you journey through this life, you have been charged to produce the evidence of being a believer.

Gustav Dore, the famous artist, lost his passport while traveling in Europe. He was at a certain boundary post between two countries and the officer in charge asked him for his passport. Dore fumbled about and finally announced, "I have lost my passport, but it is all right. I'm Dore, the artist. Please let me go in."

The officer replied, "Oh, no. We have plenty of people representing themselves as this or that great person! Here is a pencil and paper. Now, if you are Dore, the artist, prove it by drawing me a picture!"

Dore took the pencil and drew some pictures of scenes in the immediate area.

"Now, I am perfectly sure that you are Dore. No one else could draw like that!" said the officer as he allowed the great artist to enter the country.

So it is with professing followers of Christ. You say you are a Christian. But can you really produce evidence?—SOURCE UNKNOWN

12–228

WITNESS–WITNESSING

1 Peter 2:11-12

A Life-Impacting Faith

(POSB, Note 3, point 2)

Is your faith seen by unbelievers as some religious game or is it seen as your life? Are honesty and integrity seen in your faith? Does your faith really make a difference in the eyes of the lost? Listen closely to this story about a faith that made a difference.

A leading actor was honored at a banquet. In the after-dinner ceremonies the actor was asked to recite for the pleasure of his guests. He consented, and asked if there was anything special anyone in the audience would like to hear.

There was a moment's pause, and then an old clergyman spoke up. "Could you, sir," he said, "recite the twenty-third Psalm?"

A strange look came over the actor's face, but he was speechless for only a moment. "I can, sir—and I will, on one condition, and that is that after I have recited, you, my friend, will do the same."

"I?" replied the surprised clergyman; "but I am not [a public speaker]. However, if you wish, I will do so."

Impressively the great actor began the Psalm, holding his audience spellbound. As he finished, a great burst of applause broke from the guests.

After the applause had ceased, the old clergyman arose. The audience sat in intense silence. The Psalm was recited, and when it was done, there was not the slightest ripple of applause, but those in the audience whose eyes were yet dry had their heads bowed.

The great actor, with hand on the shoulder of the old clergyman, his voice trembling, exclaimed, "I reached your eyes and ears, my friends, this man reached your hearts; I know the twenty-third Psalm, this man knows the Shepherd."[95]

Is your faith real enough to cause others to want the Shepherd, too?

12–229

WITNESS-WITNESSING

1 John 4:7-21

(POSB, Note 2, point 3)

The Proof of Love

Think about this for a moment: How do you know God loves you? As you give this question some thought, here is a short story that will add some color to your imagination.

Many years ago a man found himself hiking in a mountain wilderness. Far from civilization, he was lost and he knew it. What began as a miscalculation back at the home base station had grown into a dangerous adventure. As he hiked back in a direction that looked correct, he noticed over his shoulder smoke billowing from the forest. "Wildfire!" The hiker quickened his pace as he began to worry about the oncoming fire.

What would he do? He was lost and the fire would eventually consume him. After an hour had gone by, he came to the edge of a great divide. Below him was a deep ravine. On the other side was safety. But getting across was impossible. As he walked further down the edge of the ravine, he noticed that a great tree had fallen and bridged the two sides. This was his way to escape certain death: to walk across the tree and reach the other side.

In the same sense, we were saved from destruction by God's love for us. Now, we see others lost and the eternal fires of hell coming ever closer to consume them. God had mercy on you as He placed a great tree—the cross of Christ—over the great divide between man's sin and God's holiness. In love, we, too, must show others the way to be saved. Each one must be led to the cross.

Loving others proves that you have accepted God's love—the provision of His Son who died for your sins. And there is no greater way to show your love for others than to show them the way of escape—the way of the cross.

12–230

WITNESS–WITNESSING

1 Peter 3:1-6

(POSB, Note 5)

The Testimony of Our Lives

The pages of history show that many Christian wives lead their husbands to the Lord. In each and every case, the key is a woman who is willing to *live* what she believes.

---

95 Herbert V. Prochnow. *A Treasury of Inspiration: Illustrations, Quotations, Poems and Selections.* (Grand Rapids, MI: Baker Book House, 1993), pp.112–213.

On one occasion, a small group of men were concluding their weekly Bible study. At the time, they were sharing their thoughts about all the different translations.

The first man said, "I'll stick with the good old King James Version. It has always been my favorite." The next man said, "I can't understand that old English. The New American Standard is my choice for translation."

The third man was a recent believer. "My favorite translation is my wife. Her life translated the gospel into a language I could understand."

What a great testimony! Living out the Word in a way that bears the fruit of salvation!

12–231

WORD OF GOD

1 Peter 2:1-3

(POSB, Note 2, point 3)

The Great Value of God's Word

What would you do if someone told you there was hidden treasure in your house? You would undoubtedly want to know where and what it was. As this story illustrates, the treasure is at your fingertips.

A Christian worker entered a wretched, poverty-stricken home. Beneath a rickety table, he saw a dust-covered Bible. As he left, he said, "There's a treasure in this house which if discovered and believed would make you all rich!" A diligent search was made for the hidden treasure. "Could it be a jewel or a pot of gold left by the former occupants of the home?" asked the searchers one of another. Their search was in vain. No treasure was found.

Not long thereafter, the mother picked up the old Bible. She began to [turn] the pages of the unread Bible. On the flyleaf were written these words, "Thy testimonies are better to me than thousands of gold and silver!" "Ah!" she exclaimed, "can this be the treasure the stranger spoke of?" She and the other members of the family began to read the Bible. A change came into their lives. A change came into their home. Love, joy, and peace came into hearts which were formerly filled with sin and discontentment.

When the Christian worker returned to the home, the grateful family exclaimed, "We have found the treasure, and in reading it and receiving it into our hearts, we have also found the Saviour!"[96]

The Word of God is the greatest treasure you could ever possess. Have you laid claim to your treasure...or are you living in poverty?

---

96 Walter B. Knight. *Knight's Treasury of 2,000 Illustrations*, pp.19-20.

12–232

WORD OF GOD

2 Peter 1:16-21

(POSB, Note 3, point 2)

Obeying God's Word

It is one thing to memorize certain verses in the Bible. It is another to obey what you memorize.

> There is a story of a missionary in Korea who had a visit from a native convert who lived a hundred miles away, and who walked four days to reach the mission station. The pilgrim recited proudly, without a single mistake, the whole of the Sermon on the Mount. The missionary was delighted, but he felt that he ought to warn the man that memorizing was not enough—that it was necessary to practice the words as well as to memorize them.
>
> The Korean's face lit up with happy smiles. "That is the way I learned it," he said. "I tried to memorize it, but it wouldn't stick. So I hit upon this plan—I would memorize a verse and then find a heathen neighbor of mine and practice it on him. Then I found it would stick."[97]

Scripture is the guideline for a believer's life. Are you just *reading* the Bible or are you *heeding* it?

12–233

WORD OF GOD

1 John 2:12–14

(POSB, Note 2, point 3)

Our Source of Spiritual Strength

Overconfidence in human strength has been the ruin of many. The believer needs to constantly be reminded that without an infusion of God's power, spiritual strength is not possible. Listen to this story.

> J. Wilbur Chapman once came to F. B. Meyer with the question, "What is the matter with me? So many times I seem half empty, and so many times utterly powerless; what is the matter?"
>
> He put his hand on Chapman's shoulder and answered, "Have you ever tried to breathe out three times without breathing in once?" Thinking it might be some new breathing exercise, Chapman answered, "I do not think I have." "Well," said Meyer, "try it." So he breathed out once, and then he had to breathe in again.
>
> "Don't you know," said Dr. Meyer, "that you must always breathe in before you breathe out, and that your breathing out is in proportion to your breathing in?"
>
> We must always fill the reservoir by prayer and a meditative study of the Word before we can draw out for service.[98]

Inhale God's Word... exhale spiritual strength.... Inhale God's Word... exhale spiritual strength: that is the key to a growing relationship with the Lord.

---

97 *Earnest Worker.* Walter B. Knight. *Knight's Master Book of 4,000 Illustrations*, pp.26-27.

98 *The Evangelist.* Walter B. Knight. *Knight's Treasury of 2,000 Illustrations*, pp.60-61.

12–234

WORD OF GOD

1 John 2:18-23

Protection Against Deadly Doctrine

(POSB, Note 3, point 2)

God has given the believer the great provision of His protection against antichrists or false teachers. Listen to this miraculous story.

A lieutenant in the United States Army on some far-off battle front and his buddy were sent off on an important mission. When the enemy discovered them, the lieutenant faced them, saying to himself, "Lord, it's your responsibility now."

As he reached for his carbine, a shot from one of them struck him in the breast and blasted him down. Thinking he was dead, his pal grabbed his carbine and blasted away with both guns. He received three bullet wounds, but when he finished not one of the enemy was left.

The lieutenant wrote his sister in Pennsylvania: "He was amazed when I rolled over and tried to get up. The force of that bullet had only stunned me. Dazedly, wondering why, I pulled my Bible out of my pocket and in utter muteness looked at the ugly hole in the cover. It had ripped through Genesis, Exodus, Leviticus, Numbers, and kept going. Where do you think it stopped? In the middle of the Ninety-first Psalm, pointing like a finger at this verse, **A thousand shall fall at thy side, and ten thousand shall fall at thy right hand; but it shall not come nigh thee**. I did not know such a verse was in the Bible....In utter humility I said, 'Thank You, precious God.' "[99]

This soldier was fortunate. But you, too, can protect your heart from a false teacher's deadly bullet if you hide God's Word in your heart.

12–235

WORK

1 Peter 2:18-20

Giving Your Best for the Lord

(POSB, Note 1)

At work, believers too often yield to the temptation to slack off and offer only *marginal* work to their employer. But every Christian's work should be rated by his or her employer as *excellent*.

[Football coach,] Gene Stallings tells of an incident when he was defensive backfield coach of the Dallas Cowboys. Two All-Pro players, Charlie Waters and Cliff Harris, were sitting in front of their lockers after playing a tough game against the Washington Redskins. They were still in their uniforms, and their heads were bowed in exhaustion. Waters said to Harris, "By the way Cliff, what was the final score?"

As these men show, excellence isn't determined by comparing our score to someone else's. Excellence comes from giving one's best, no matter the score.[100]

As a believer, you should be giving your best for the Lord at *all* times and in *all* circumstances.

---

99 From leaflet, "A Lieutenant's Miraculous Escape." Walter B. Knight. *Knight's Master Book of 4,000 Illustrations*, pp.526-527.

100 Craig B. Larson, Editor. *Illustrations for Preaching & Teaching*, p.73.

12–236

WORK

1 Peter 2:18-20

(POSB, Note 4)

Searching for God's Blessings

How we work paints a very sharp image of our character. If we work hard and perform well, God will bless our efforts. One of Aesop's fables illustrates this point for us.

THE FARMER AND HIS SONS

> A farmer, being at death's door, and desiring to impart to his sons a secret of much moment, called them round him and said, "My sons, I am shortly about to die. I would have you know, therefore, that in my vineyard there lies a hidden treasure. Dig, and you will find it." As soon as their father was dead, the sons took spade and fork and turned up the soil of the vineyard over and over again, in their search for the treasure which they supposed to lie buried there. They found none, however: but the vines, after so thorough a digging, produced a crop such as had never before been seen.
>
> [The moral:] There is no treasure without toil.[101]

Work like there is a treasure waiting for you, because there is! The treasure is God's acceptance and reward.

12–237

WORLDLINESS

1 John 4:1-6

(POSB, Note 4, point 2)

Deadly Necessities

It has been said "birds of a feather flock together." This simply means that people of the same nature congregate together. In the same way, people who follow false teachers have attached themselves to worldly weights.

> In Jules Verne's novel *The Mysterious Island*, he tells of five men who escape a Civil War prison camp by hijacking a hot air balloon. As they rise into the air, they realize the wind is carrying them over the ocean. Watching their homeland disappear on the horizon, they wonder how much longer the balloon can stay aloft.
>
> As the hours pass and the surface of the ocean draws closer, the men decide they must cast overboard some of the weight, for they had no way to heat the air in the balloon. Shoes, overcoats, and weapons are reluctantly discarded, and the uncomfortable aviators feel their balloon rise. But only temporarily. Soon they find themselves dangerously close to the waves again, so they toss their food. Better to be high and hungry than drown on a full belly!
>
> Unfortunately, this, too, is only a temporary solution, and the craft again threatens to lower the men into the sea. One man has an idea: they can tie the ropes that hold the passenger car and sit on those ropes. Then they can cut away the basket beneath

101 William J. Bennett. *The Book of Virtues.* (New York, NY: Simon & Schuster, 1993), p.370.

them. As they sever the very thing they had been standing on, it drops into the ocean, and the balloon rises.

Not a minute too soon, they spot land. Eager to stand on terra firma again, the five jump into the water and swim to the island. They live, spared because they were able to discern the difference between what really was needed and what was not. The "necessities" they once thought they couldn't live without were the very weights that almost cost them their lives.[102]

The best advice you can give someone who is following a false teacher is to *abandon ship* and cling to the Rock, the Lord Jesus Christ.

12–238

WORLDLINESS

1 John 2:7-11

Hatred Is Blind

(POSB, Note 4, point 2)

There are many men who live in darkness, accumulating material goods, but not seeing the value of the person next to them. Listen to the "accomplishments" of some men whose love of money was more valuable to them than human life.

In 1923 a group of the world's most successful financiers met at the Edgewater Beach Hotel in Chicago.

Collectively, these tycoons controlled more wealth than there was in the United States Treasury, and for years newspapers and magazines had been printing their success stories and urging the youth of the nation to follow their examples.

Twenty-seven years later, let's see what happened to them.

(1) CHARLES SCHWAB—the president of the largest independent steel company—lived on borrowed money the last five years of his life, and died penniless.

(2) ARTHUR CUTTEN—the greatest wheat speculator—died abroad [unable to pay his bills].

(3) RICHARD WHITNEY—the president of the New York Stock Exchange—was released ... from Sing Sing [prison].

(4) ALBERT FALL—the member of the President's Cabinet—was pardoned from prison so he could die at home.

(5) JESSE LIVERMORE—the greatest bear in Wall Street—committed suicide.

(6) LEON FRASER—the president of the Bank of International Settlement—committed suicide.

(7) IVAR KRUEGER—the head of the world's greatest monopoly—committed suicide.[103]

All of these men had learned how to make money, but not one of them had learned how to live.

---

102 Craig B. Larson. *Illustrations for Preaching and Teaching*, p.113.

103 Paul Lee Tan. *Encyclopedia of 7,700 Illustrations: Signs of the Times*, p.824.

12–239

WORLDLINESS

1 Peter 2:1-3

(POSB, Intro)

Our Desperate Need for Cleansing

Have you ever been tempted to do something *halfway*, doing just enough to get the job done?

Many people like to give a favorite piece of furniture or keepsake a new look, a fresh coat of paint. However, sometimes, instead of stripping off the old finish, they choose to save some time by simply hiding the old paint, along with its problems, with a fresh coat. As they repaint, they ignore the cracked and dirty surface. Their motto is "Out of sight, out of mind." They just paint over the mess, trying to make it look good without taking the necessary steps to produce a quality piece of work. But in time their sloppy effort betrays them when the new coat of paint begins to bubble and peel off.

In the same sense, we have been charged by God to strip away the old surface of carnality before we apply the Word of God to our lives. If the believer attempts to paint over his old life of sin without first removing the dirt and shame, his efforts will prove to be wasted.

Topical Index

ACKNOWLEDGMENTS

Every child of God is precious to the Lord and deeply loved. And every child as a servant of the Lord touches the lives of those who come in contact with him or his ministry. The writing ministries of the following servants have touched this work, and we are grateful that God brought their writings our way. We hereby acknowledge their ministries, being fully aware that there are many others whose writings have touched our lives and who deserve mention but whose names have faded from memory. May our wonderful Lord continue to bless the ministries of these dear servants—and the ministries of us all—as we diligently labor to reach the world for Christ and to meet the desperate needs of those who suffer so much.

ACKNOWLEDGMENTS AND BIBLIOGRAPHY

Alice in Wonderland. (Walt Disney, 1951), directed by Hamilton Luske and Clyde Geronimi. As quoted in PreachingToday.com.

Barclay, William. *The Letters of James and Peter.* "Daily Study Bible Series." Philadelphia, PA, Westminster Press.

Barnhouse, Donald Grey. *Let Me Illustrate.* Grand Rapids, MI: Fleming H. Revell, 1967.

Bennett, William J. *The Book of Virtues.* New York, NY: Simon & Schuster, 1993.

Duewel, Wesley L. *Touch the World Through Prayer.* Grand Rapids, MI: Francis Asbury Press, 1986.

God's Little Devotional Book. Tulsa, OK: Honor Books, Inc., 1995.

Gray, Alice. *More Stories for the Heart.* Sisters, OR: Multnomah Press, 1997.

Green, Michael P. *Illustrations for Biblical Preaching.* Grand Rapids, MI: Baker Books, 1996.

Hybels, Bill. *Honest To God?* Grand Rapids, MI: Zondervan Publishing House, 1990.

Hybels, Bill & Mark Mittleberg. *Becoming a Contagious Christian.* Grand Rapids, MI: Zondervan Publishing House, 1994.

Keller, W. Phillip. *A Shepherd Looks at Psalm 23.* Grand Rapids, MI: Zondervan Publishing House, 1979.

Knight, Walter B. *3,000 Illustrations for Christian Service.* Grand Rapids, MI: Eerdmans Publishing Company, 1971.

———. *Knight's Master Book of 4,000 Illustrations.* Grand Rapids, MI: Eerdmans Publishing Co., 1994.

———. *Knight's Treasury of 2,000 Illustrations.* Grand Rapids, MI: Eerdmans Publishing Company, 1992.

Krivohalavek, Ken. *Rejoicin' an' Repentin'.* Olathe, KS: KLK Ministries, 2002.

Kyle, Ted and John Todd. *A Treasury of Bible Illustrations.* Chattanooga, TN: AMG International, 1995.

Larson, Craig B., Editor. *Choice Contemporary Stories & Illustrations for Preachers, Teachers & Writers.* Grand Rapids, MI: Baker Books, 1998.

———. *Illustrations for Preaching & Teaching.* Grand Rapids, MI: Baker Books, 1993.

Leadership Journal. Carol Stream, IL: *Christianity Today.*

Lucado, Max. *And the Angels Were Silent.* Portland, OR: Multnomah Press, 1992.

———. *He Still Moves Stones.* Dallas, TX: Word Publishing, 1993.

———. *In the Grip of Grace.* Dallas, TX: Word Publishing, 1996.

———. *When God Whispers Your Name.* Dallas, TX: Word Publishing, 1994.

Mains, Karen. *Open Heart, Open Home.* Elgin, Ill: David C. Cook Publishing Co., 1976.

Prochnow, Herbert V. *A Treasury of Inspiration: Illustrations, Quotations, Poems and Selections.* Grand Rapids, MI: Baker Book House, 1993.

Reed, John W., Editor. *1100 Illustrations from the Writings of D. L. Moody.* Grand Rapids, MI: Baker Book House, 1996.

Santana's Wayward Spirituality. Preaching Today.com.

Singspiration. Division of Zondervan Corporation, Nashville, TN, 1932.

Tan, Paul Lee. *Encyclopedia of 7,700 Illustrations: Signs of the Times.* Rockville, MD: Assurance Publishers, 1985.

———. *Encyclopedia of 15,000 Illustrations.* Dallas, TX: Bible Communications, Inc., 1998.

White, Robert. *Life in the Spirit.* Minsk, Belarus: Spirit Life Books, 2000.

Wiersbe, Warren W. *The Bible Exposition Commentary, Vol.2.* Wheaton, IL: Victor Books, 1989.

Zodhiates, Spiros, Th.D. *Illustrations of Bible Truths.* Chattanooga, TN: AMG International, 1995.

Outline Bible Resources

This material, like similar works, has come from imperfect man and is thus susceptible to human error. We are nevertheless grateful to God for both calling us and empowering us through His Holy Spirit to undertake this task. Because of His goodness and grace, ***The Preacher's Outline & Sermon Bible***® New Testament is complete, and Old Testament volumes are releasing periodically.

The Minister's Personal Handbook and other helpful **Outline Bible Resources** are available in printed form as well as releasing electronically on WORDsearch software.

God has given the strength and stamina to bring us this far. Our confidence is that as we keep our eyes on Him and grounded in the undeniable truths of the Word, we will continue working through the Old Testament volumes. The future includes other helpful Outline Bible Resources for God's dear servants to use in their Bible Study and discipleship.

We offer this material first to Him in whose Name we labor and serve and for whose glory it has been produced and, second, to everyone everywhere who preaches and teaches the Word.

Our daily prayer is that each volume will lead thousands, millions, yes even billions, into a better understanding of the Holy Scriptures and a fuller knowledge of Jesus Christ the Incarnate Word, of whom the Scriptures so faithfully testify.

You will be pleased to know that Leadership Ministries Worldwide partners with Christian organizations, printers, and mission groups around the world to make Outline Bible Resources available and affordable in many countries and foreign languages. It is our goal that *every* leader around the world, both clergy and lay, will be able to understand God's Holy Word and present God's message with more clarity, authority, and understanding—all beyond his or her own power.

LEADERSHIP MINISTRIES WORLDWIDE
PO Box 21310 • Chattanooga, TN 37424-0310
423) 855-2181 • FAX (423) 855-8616
info@outlinebible.org
www.outlinebible.org - FREE Download materials

LEADERSHIP MINISTRIES WORLDWIDE

Publishers of Outline Bible Resources

Currently Available Materials, with New Volumes Releasing Regularly

- **THE PREACHER'S OUTLINE & SERMON BIBLE® (POSB)**

NEW TESTAMENT

Matthew I (chapters 1-15)
Matthew II (chapters 16-28)
Mark
Luke
John
Acts
Romans
1 & 2 Corinthians
Galatians, Ephesians, Philippians, Colossians
1 & 2 Thess., 1 & 2 Timothy, Titus, Philemon
Hebrews, James
1 & 2 Peter, 1, 2, & 3 John, Jude
Revelation
Master Outline & Subject Index

OLD TESTAMENT

Genesis I (chapters 1-11)
Genesis II (chapters 12-50)
Exodus I (chapters 1-18)
Exodus II (chapters 19-40)
Leviticus
Numbers
Deuteronomy
Joshua
Judges, Ruth
1 Samuel
2 Samuel
1 Kings
2 Kings
1 Chronicles
2 Chronicles
Ezra, Nehemiah, Esther
Job
Proverbs
Ecclesiastes, Song of Solomon
Isaiah 1 (chapters 1-35)
Isaiah 2 (chapters 36-66)
Jeremiah 1 (chapters 1-29)
Jeremiah 2 (chapters 30-52), Lamentations
Ezekiel
Daniel/Hosea
Joel, Amos, Obadiah, Jonah, Micah, Nahum
Habakkuk, Zephaniah, Haggai, Zechariah, Malachi
New volumes release periodically

KJV Available in Deluxe 3-Ring Binders or Softbound Edition • NIV Available in Softbound Only

- **The Preacher's Outline & Sermon Bible New Testament — 3 Vol. Hardcover • KJV – NIV**
- ***What the Bible Says to the Minister* — The Minister's Personal Handbook**
  12 Chs. - 127 Subjects - 400 Verses Expounded - Italian Imitation Leather or Paperback
- **Practical Word Studies In the New Testament** — 2 Vol. Hardcover Set
- **The Teacher's Outline & Study Bible™ - Various New Testament Books**
  Complete 30 - 45 minute lessons – with illustrations and discussion questions
- **Practical Illustrations — Companion to the POSB**
  Arranged by topic and Scripture reference
- **OUTLINE New Testament with Thompson®** Chain-References
  Combines verse-by-verse outlines with the legendary Thompson References
- **What the Bible Says Series – Various Subjects**
  Prayer • The Passion • The Ten Commandments • The Tabernacle
- **Software – Various products powered by WORDsearch**
  New Testament • Pentateuch • History • Various Prophets • Practical Word Studies
- **Topical Sermons Series – Available online only**
  7 sermons per series • Sermons are from the Preacher's Outline & Sermon Bible
- **Non-English Translations of various books**
  Included languages are: Russian – Spanish – Korean – Hindi – Chinese – Bulgarian – Romanian – Malayalam – Nepali – Italian – Arabic
  • Future: French, Portuguese

— Contact LMW for Specific Language Availability and Prices —

For quantity orders and information, please contact:
LEADERSHIP MINISTRIES WORLDWIDE or Your Local Christian Bookstore
PO Box 21310 • Chattanooga, TN 37424-0310
(423) 855-2181 (9am – 5pm Eastern) • FAX (423) 855-8616
E-mail - info@outlinebible.org Order online at www.outlinebible.org

11/12

PURPOSE STATEMENT

LEADERSHIP MINISTRIES WORLDWIDE
exists to equip ministers, teachers, and laymen in their understanding, preaching and teaching of God's Word by publishing and distributing worldwide *The Preacher's Outline & Sermon Bible®* and related **Outline Bible Resources**, to reach & disciple men, women, boys and girls for Jesus Christ.

MISSION STATEMENT

1. To make the Bible so understandable – its truth so clear and plain – that men and women everywhere, whether teacher or student, preacher or hearer, can grasp its message and receive Jesus Christ as Savior, and...

2. To place the Bible in the hands of all who will preach and teach God's Holy Word, verse by verse, precept by precept, regardless of the individual's ability to purchase it.

Outline Bible Resources have been given to LMW for printing and especially distribution worldwide at/below cost, by those who remain anonymous. One fact, however, is as true today as it was in the time of Christ:

THE GOSPEL IS FREE, BUT THE COST OF TAKING IT IS NOT

LMW depends on the generous gifts of believers with a heart for Him and a love for the lost. They help pay for the printing, translating, and distributing of **Outline Bible Resources** into the hands of God's servants worldwide, who will present the Gospel message with clarity, authority, and understanding beyond their own.

LMW was incorporated in the state of Tennessee in July 1992 and received IRS 501 (c)(3) nonprofit status in March 1994. LMW is an international, nondenominational mission organization. All proceeds from USA sales, along with donations from donor partners, go directly to underwrite our translation and distribution projects of **Outline Bible Resources** to preachers, church and lay leaders, and Bible students around the world.